Barre, Vt

Please p[...]

Marilyn Miller

Gift of Marilyn

May 1960

Vestment Department

VESTMENTS AND CHURCH FURNITURE

IS VOLUME

114

OF THE

Twentieth Century Encyclopedia of Catholicism

UNDER SECTION

X

THE WORSHIP OF THE CHURCH

IT IS ALSO THE

38TH

VOLUME IN ORDER OF PUBLICATION

Edited by HENRI DANIEL-ROPS of the Académie Française

VESTMENTS AND
CHURCH FURNITURE

By ROBERT LESAGE

Translated from the French by FERGUS MURPHY

HAWTHORN BOOKS · PUBLISHERS · *New York*

First Edition, March, 1960

NIHIL OBSTAT

Joannes M. T. Barton, S.T.D., L.S.S.
Censor Deputatus

IMPRIMATUR

E. Morrogh Bernard
Vicarius Generalis

247.7   Westmonasterii, die XXVI NOVEMBRIS MCMLIX

CONTENTS

PART I

THE ALTAR AND ITS FURNITURE

THE CHURCH

Christianity has been an innovator in many ways; the form of its places of worship is but one example of this. Of course, all the ancient religions had their sacred places where the most solemn rites of their external and public worship were celebrated. But the temple was always of limited proportions and merely contained the statue of the god before which an altar was frequently erected. The Tabernacle built by Moses was only a small tent. The high priest was the only person who went inside it. The worshippers stood around it in the open air in the courts set aside for them for that purpose.

What distinguishes the Christian Church is its meeting place, a public building set apart both for divine worship and the collective prayer of the faithful.

The word *ecclesia* (church) is derived from the Greek verb meaning "convoke". It is a distinctively Christian word. It designates both the society consisting of Christ's disciples and their common house. The building, therefore, is the material embodiment of the Christian association. It is consequently quite natural that the architectural combinations of the material church and its general lay-out should represent and reflect the image of the spiritual Church.

All the faithful, being Christ's members and united to Christ, share in his sacrifice and prayer to the Father. St Augustine says:

> If it is our duty to adore God, we should offer him our services, either by means of some sacred sign or in our

person. Since taken together we are his temple and since each single one of us is his temple . . . let our heart serve as God's altar.

It becomes such when it strives to elevate itself by appeasing him through the intermediary of his only Son, our priest; when in our fight for truth, we sacrifice ourselves to him as victims even to the shedding of our blood; when we offer him a sweet incense by burning with a devout and holy love before him; when we give him back the goods which he has bestowed upon us by a total consecration of ourselves to him; when, in peaceful days, we thank him through Church solemnities for his benefits; when we offer ourselves up to him as victims of humility and praise in the fire of ardent charity on the altars of our heart.

Surely my church, where I meet my brothers and my forebears, is the most beautiful house in my little village or the finest monument in my part of the town? How sound, intelligent and pious was the rivalry shown by our fathers in building churches with their own hands as also their persistent desire to be buried beneath the flagstones of their church. Their work and mortal remains constitute an abiding presence as long as the building endures and whenever it becomes a scene of activity they come to life again.

It is not merely a question of delight of the eyes, aesthetic emotions, lessons in doctrine, the aid to contemplation, the assemblage of saints and angels, the great patterns of men, animals, constellations and flora, or even the philosophical entities and devils who hang from the fundamentally symbolical columns, walls and towers. These windows, recesses, frescoes, radial chapels, are forms of all the arts which meet in the house of God. They are eternal forms skilfully evoked by artisans and artists in stone, glass and cement.

If it is true that a church should not be a museum or an exhibition hall it is truer still that a sacred building should not shelter what would not even be tolerated in an ordinary drawing-room. Adaptations and innovations must be carried out in a spirit of obedience governed by wisdom.

We should meditate on these words of Pius XII, taken from his encyclical *Musicae sacrae* of Christmas 1955:

> Hence the artist who has no faith, or whose heart and conduct are far from God, should not in any way apply himself to religious art, for he lacks that interior vision needed to perceive what God's majesty and worship demand. Nor can he hope that his works, empty of religious inspiration, will infuse that faith and devotion befitting the sacred house of God, and hence worthy of being admitted by the Church, guardian as she is and judge of religious life, even though such works will reveal an artist who is skilful and endowed with superficial ability.

CHAPTER I

THE ALTAR

The altar is the focal point of the whole Christian temple. The latter is built to shelter the altar around which the clergy and faithful assemble. What is the first thing we see on entering a Catholic church? The altar, the high-altar, the great altar which from time immemorial has been the material expression of worship, the indispensable instrument of sacrifice. It was invented by man even before he dreamed of building temples to the divinity. Wherever a sacrifice and a priesthood exist there also we find an altar.

The very connotation of altar indicates a raised place: *altus*, high; *alta res*, a raised thing; *alto*, raise, cause to grow. It is a monument raised above ground level and destined to receive the victim to be sacrificed. It is the place reserved for the offering of the sacrifice. It is a horizontal surface on which the thing to be offered is laid: the officiant takes the chosen victim from the ground, lifts it up to his own height and then places it on the altar, between earth and heaven.

In Christian parlance the Fathers of the Church avoided the use of the word *ara*, which had acquired a traditionally pagan flavour. They preferred the words *altar*, *altare* (and *altarium* in low Latin) which are regularly found in the liturgy. Neither the pagan altars, so varied in shape, nor the Hebrew altar had any real influence on the Christian altar. A new sacrifice called for new ideas and the first Christians were necessarily inspired by the Last Supper which Jesus took in company with his disciples.

THE CHRISTIAN ALTAR IS A TABLE

For the celebration of Mass the apostles used the tables which they found in private houses where they were staying. These tables were of different shapes—rectangular, semicircular or tripod. The famous fresco of "the breaking of bread", in the Priscillian cemetery at Rome, dates back to the beginning of the second century. It is the oldest representation of the holy sacrifice. Six persons are seated, side by side, at a long semicircular table. In the centre the priest is breaking a loaf of bread marked with a cross, nearby is a chalice with two handles. On the other hand, in one of the chapels of "the sacraments" in St Callistus' cemetery, the communion table is distinct from that which serves as an altar. The latter is shaped like a tripod and holds the loaves. These tripods were probably in general use because they were easy to transport.

Indeed, we read in the *Liber pontificalis* that Felix I ordered "Masses to be said on the tombs of the martyrs" which merely seems to have been the sanction of a custom that had been in force a long time. Now, it is said that celebration took place directly on the tombstones of the saints, under the *arcosolia* of the catacombs. But these arcosoles, arches hollowed out in the subsoil over the tombs, would scarcely allow this mode of celebration. Rather was it *near* the tombs and *against* them on tables brought there that the celebration took place.

Later on, the sepulchre of the martyrs itself sometimes served as an altar. In the basilicas erected over the cemeteries, it was called *confessio-altar*. The venerated tomb was not displaced, it remained in the crypt, and above it, at ground level, a stone altar was raised. Nearby, stairs gave easy access to the vault in order that the faithful might descend under the altar and venerate the *memoria*, the *martyrium* or the *confessio* at close quarters.

The bodies of the martyrs themselves taken from their

primitive tombs were laid beside the altars: very often behind them, and sometimes also between the supports of the altar table. Whence the altar-shrine and, in the sixteenth century in Italy, the sarcophagus-altars where the primitive form of table is completely replaced by a tomb, whose slab forms the *mensa*. Former use of the table-altar has often left its mark in the shape of four small columns placed at the corners of the structure.

This historical outline enables us to understand the great variety of our altars. All the forms mentioned still exist today but we must admit that for the past thirty years it is the table-altar which now prevails. In almost all new churches, the *mensa* is a fine natural stone supported on a big block, or two pillars or four columns, which are also of stone.

The reredos, placed behind the altars since the time of the Middle Ages, is no longer in fashion. The gradines themselves are completely abolished and the candlesticks are placed directly on the cloth. This is preferable. The only objects remaining on the altar are those absolutely indispensable to the holy sacrifice—crucifix, candlesticks, missal and altar cards.

The altar-table also corresponded with the desire to celebrate "facing the people" which began to appear about the year 1930. Mgr Harscouët adopted this usage in his Chartres Cathedral and Cardinal Verdier did so at Notre-Dame de Paris. This sufficed to bring about the adoption of this ancient provision in France and Belgium.

There was no need to request permission since it was explicitly indicated in the rubrics of the Missal—"If the altar is orientated, or turned towards the people, in such a way that the celebrant has his face turned towards the people, he does not turn his back to the altar to say *Dominus vobiscum, Orate fratres, Ite, missa est,* nor to impart the blessing; but, when he has kissed the middle of the altar, he extends and joins his hands, as above, salutes the people and gives the blessing."

Far from being a privilege reserved to the pope, as the expression "Roman altar" might lead one to believe, this is an arrangement that may be freely adopted.

It has certain advantages but is also somewhat inconvenient, especially as regards the position of the tabernacle. Instead of making a low tabernacle, a little higher than the ciboriums used, some have thought they should place this tabernacle in the pillars or on supports away from the altar. Such methods have again been forbidden by the Congregation of Rites in 1957, as well as celebration "facing the people" in churches with only one altar.

CONSECRATION OF THE ALTAR

Providing that its table and support are of natural stone, the former in a single block, every altar may be consecrated. It is called a fixed altar because the obligation exists to seal the *mensa* to the *stipites* and not because it is fixed to the ground in an immovable manner.

Consecrated stones are movable altars which, in the absence of fixed altars, may be placed on wooden furniture in the form of an altar, on tables erected for this purpose, and even on improvised supports as army chaplains or soldier-priests are obliged to do. These are small stones, sufficiently large, however, to accommodate the chalice, the paten and the ciborium used for the holy sacrifice. They must be consecrated, like fixed altars, by a bishop, but according to a simplified rite.

The consecration of a fixed altar is one of the most moving and solemn ceremonies of Catholic worship. It is obligatory every time that the bishop consecrates a church. It may also be done separately apart from the dedication of the building itself.

The bishop mixes and blesses special water in order to trace five little crosses in the middle and at the corners, on the *mensa*, then he performs numerous purifications by sprinkling all the parts of the altar. He goes round it seven times, while the *Asperges* and the psalm *Miserere* are being chanted: "Thou wilt sprinkle me with a wand of hyssop, and I shall be clean; washed, and I shall be whiter than snow."

The clergy then form a procession and go to the chapel where the relics have been placed. The sacred remains of the chosen martyrs are carried by the pontiff himself or, if they are of some size, on a bier by two priests wearing chasubles. This transportation is like a funeral cortège marked by joyful Christian hope. Do not these saints whose bones are with us already enjoy heavenly bliss? Are they not united to Christ in the beatific vision before being associated with him in the sacrifice of the altar?

The bishop places the casket containing the precious relics in a little sepulchre cut out of the face of the *mensa* and previously anointed with holy chrism. He incenses them and, assisted by a mason, seals the stone lid. If this lid is removed or broken, the whole consecration must be renewed. Finally, the bishop anoints the table of the altar, the front edge of this stone and then its four corners where it is secured by cement to its support.

The burning of twenty-five grains of incense on the table on which the holy oils have been abundantly applied, gives the impression of a burning altar ready for its victims. This offering of perfumes indeed precedes the real sacrifice of the New Law—the first celebration of Mass on this consecrated altar.

VISITING THE ALTARS

Canon Crampon was right, when commenting on the twentieth chapter of Exodus (where Moses speaks of the altar of sacrifices) he said: "The altar represents man striving to raise himself up to the throne of God in heaven; God descends upon it in order to communicate with man."

This is the reason for our great respect for altars. We need not wonder, therefore, if chosen souls, especially during the Middle Ages, looked upon the devotional practice of visiting altars as a form of asceticism. Contemplation accompanied by vigils and countless genuflections was well designed to subdue the body.

This devotion is attributed to St Benedict of Aniane († 831), but it is certainly older than the great reformer. We frequently find the following expressions used by hagiographers when referring to visiting of altars: "making the round of the altars in prayer" or "genuflecting around the altars".

The *Vita* of St Gervinus († 1075), abbot of Saint-Riquier in Ponthieu (Somme), informs us of the classic manner of visiting the altars. Nightly vigils, going around the altars while praying, weeping, genuflecting and reciting psalms, were the most typical forms of this devotion as understood by the monks in the second half of the eleventh century.

Besides, St Gervinus' piety was probably connected with his veneration for saints' relics. For when he was appointed abbot the monastery already possessed thirty altars; in his turn he installed a crypt and there placed four new altars embellished with numerous relics.

Another motive underlay the spread of this devotion throughout Europe. The chief reformers of monastic and canonical life, such as St Romuald and St Chrodegang, forbade, under pain of excommunication, anyone to go back to bed after Matins. The religious therefore exercised their ingenuity to find various ways of passing these silent hours for their souls' profit. Dom Couneson writing in the *Revue liturgique et monastique* states: "First, they recited their favourite psalms, sometimes going through the whole Psalter; then they walked in the cloisters sunk in devout meditation or else went to the chapterhouse to read some passages of the Scripture or the Fathers. If sleep threatened to overcome them they rose and started making the rounds of the altars, sprinkling themselves frequently and not sparing the holy water."

St Thomas Becket, archbishop of Canterbury, was warned on December 28th, 1170, that the royal emissaries had been ordered to put him to death on the following day. He retired to take a few moments' rest and, early in the morning, went down to the cathedral to hear Mass. As was his habit he then went to kneel successively at the foot of all the altars in the basilica, invoking the saints to whom he was specially devoted and saying countless and fervent prayers before their reliquaries or their tombs. He could easily have fled, but he feared to lose the opportunity of martyrdom. After dinner, the four assassins besieged the monastery. The religious prevailed upon Thomas to come to Vespers in order to shut himself up in the church where they thought he would be safer. The executioners, having forced their way into the cloister, rushed furiously into the church and shouted like madmen: "Where is Thomas Becket? Where is the archbishop? Where is this traitor to king and state?" Then the saint, who was quite undismayed, appeared and said: "Here I am, not a traitor to the state, but a priest of Jesus Christ." One of the assassins said to him: "Fly, or else you die." He wished to get him out of the church in order to avoid killing him in such a holy place. They tried their best to drag him away, but failing in their attempt, one of them struck him on the head with a sword. His three companions did likewise, cleaving his skull in two so that his brains were spattered over his face.

The presence of martyrs' relics and the celebration of the holy sacrifice are not the altar's sole claims on our deep veneration. Its symbolism endows it with an incomparable nobility. Is it not in truth the *image of Christ himself*? It is like God living in the midst of his people.

That is why the bishop says to the acolytes whom he is going to ordain subdeacons, since one of their functions is the washing of the sacred linen, "As witnessed by John, who in his Apocalypse states that he saw a golden altar

set before the throne, the altar of holy Church is Christ
himself. In and by him the sacrifices of the faithful are
consecrated to God the Father. The cloths and corporals
of this altar are Christ's members, that is to say, God's
faithful by whom Christ is enwrapped as in costly apparel."

The altar is symbolical of Christ because it is of stone
and stone is a biblical figure of Jesus, "the corner-
stone" of the Church, according to St Paul's saying. On
earth he offered himself in his humanity which he delivered
up to death and this humanity is, so to speak, the altar on
which the supreme Pontiff sacrifices. The five crosses engraved on its table represent our Saviour's five wounds.
The table itself is purified by numerous ablutions because
it represents the eternal Pontiff of the New Testament who
was "holy, innocent and stainless". It is anointed several
times because it is the emblem of him of whom it is written:
"The Spirit of the Lord rests upon me, by whom he hath
anointed me". This is what is meant by the phrase used in
the Roman pontifical: *Altare Christus est* (The altar is
Christ).

The altar also symbolizes the unity of the priesthood
and of the Church. In early days there was a certain cult
of the unity of the altar which is still the usual practice
among oriental Christians. During the first centuries there
was only one altar for each meeting-place. As thus laid
down the principle is still in force if every secondary chapel
in a church is regarded as a separate meeting-place. It is
principally moral unity that is here in question.

There is a single priest from whom the Father accepts
sacrifices and who stands out among us as head over his
members. Optatus of Milevis in order to designate the
schismatical movement which broke out in Carthage in
312 against the lawful bishop Cecilius could find nothing
stronger to say than "altar has been raised up against
altar".

For God has willed the unity of all his children in common obedience to a single Pastor. Outside this visible unity there can be no Church. This is the favourite theme of St Ignatius of Antioch: "Have only a single Eucharist because the flesh of our Lord Jesus is one, as is his chalice through union with his Blood. The altar is one as is also the bishop with his priests and deacons. Nothing is good unless it be done in unity—you all hasten to come together in God's temple, as on a single altar, that is to say on the only Jesus Christ."

CHAPTER II

THE CRUCIFIX

It seems quite natural to us on entering a church that the first thing we see is the image of Christ crucified occupying the place of honour in a prominent position above the high altar and indeed raised higher than anything else in the building. It is quite normal for Catholics to raise aloft the standard of the new Law, the cross, which reminds us that the sacrifice of Mass offered on the altar is the same as that of Calvary.

But it was not always so. The first Christians did not wish to display the cross while the cult of idols was still practised. The catechumens, who were not as yet well enough grounded in their faith, might have been led to confuse the duly recommended reverence of the image with its adoration which had been rightly forbidden.

Being unable to interpret God's word "Cast no metal to make thyself images", the Jews would have been scandalized and turned away from a religion which they would have considered repugnant to Yahweh's most formal commands. Besides, crucifixion was a torture introduced into their land by the hated invader. The pagans themselves detested this punishment which was certainly the most degrading of all and was reserved for slaves.

After Constantine's conversion the cross ceased to be an object of shame. It was no longer used as an instrument of torture, the emperor's famous *labarum* was cruciform surmounted by the first two Greek letters of Christ's name,

X and P, enclosed in a crown of glory. Moreover, when his mother St Helena discovered the true cross, Christians everywhere adopted it as their sign and it became the object of a real devotion.

"However, people very seldom dared to represent in sculpture or painting the features of the crucified divinity upon it", writes Canon Duret. "In their place some symbols were added to the empty cross: a divine haloed hand piercing a cloud, a recumbent lamb *tanquam occisus*: it was surmounted by a medallion of Christ."

The crucifix proper did not make its appearance until some time in the fifth century. The two oldest Christian documents date from this period; one is a sculpture in wood on the doors of St Sabina in Rome, the other an ivory preserved in the British Museum, London.

According to several historians John VII, elected in 705, was the first pope to sanction the use of the crucifix. Jesus is shown on it, living and impassible, with a gentle gracious countenance and clothed in a long mantle with sleeves, or *colobium*. "Those whom nakedness offended", says Dom Leclercq, "took no account of the spectacle offered by Calvary, they were solely concerned with avoiding a representation which shocked them."

Since the mystery of the cross is that of our Saviour's sovereignty the artists of the fifth century readily decked out the crucifix in royal apparel. Jesus is crowned either with a royal diadem or else with a flowering crown which was the crown of honour in medieval heraldry. These crosses were therefore embellished with rich decoration and treated with really aesthetic munificence: ivory, brass and precious metals were used and were often encrusted with stones or uncut gems of various hues.

The western world shrank from the horror of the reality of crucifixion, but from the eleventh century Jesus' robe grew shorter, the sleeves disappeared and four nails supported his body: one in each hand and one in each foot.

During the thirteenth century the royal crown was replaced by the crown of thorns which thenceforward encircled Christ's forehead bent earthwards. His face is sorrowful, his physical sufferings have marked his thin shrunken body, his arms are no longer at right angles to his torso, a mere scrap of material or even loin-cloth hides his nakedness.

This tendency towards realism became increasingly evident with the result that in the fifteenth century the crucifix assumed all the features of human nature subjected to the most fearful torture. In place of the former impression of the triumph of the divinity on the cross artists evoked a feeling of compassion in the minds of the faithful.

THE ALTAR CROSS

It is very difficult to establish a date for the appearance of the crucifix on altars. "The offering alone", says Cardinal Schuster, "was placed on the sacred table which was covered with a plain cloth at the moment of sacrifice so that it might be laid, as it were, in God's very bosom. The altar, therefore, could not possibly serve as a resting place for cross, candlesticks or other objects."

Ancient documents first show the chalice, the bread, the paten, then the Missal, and occasionally a cross hung in the centre or on the sides of the *ciborium* which was a baldaquin supported by columns and designed to shelter the altar. After the Carolingian period this *crux pensilis* gave place to the processional cross which was fixed to the altar at the beginning of the eucharistic sacrifice.

The *Ordo Romanus XI*, of the twelfth century, informs us that the processional cross is carried at the head of the cortège which goes to the stational basilica and on arrival there the subdeacon places it on the altar. The upper part of this movable cross was soon arranged to fit both the processional staff and the socket set up on the altar to receive it.

Real crucifixes, furnished with quadrangular or more often triangular bases, next appear. In the fourteenth century they attained considerable size and importance. They were no longer placed on the altars for a few hours only but became permanent fixtures.

They were made of red copper and the eyes of Christ are in blue glass; they are found more often in wood ornamented with paintings and gildings or carved and set in a mount of pearls and enamels, or simply painted and framed. "And in order that they might attract the glances of the faithful," said Hoppenot, "as well as the priest's, they were raised up on steps, while awaiting a later age when they were to be enthroned over the tabernacle itself. The crucifix, which, after so many vicissitudes, had won its place on the altar, was never to leave it—and the day was dawning when the rubrics would order the priest not to pronounce the name of Jesus at the altar without turning and bowing respectfully towards the cross to which Jesus is nailed."

The altar cross should be of large dimensions in order to be seen by all. In 1746 Benedict XIV condemned the use of too small crosses: "The placing of a cross which is too small before a statue or a picture violates the laws of the Church", he wrote.

Certain arrangements accepted by last-century or contemporary artists must therefore be regarded as real errors, for instance, gigantic candlesticks surrounding a barely visible and miserable little cross; there is even to be observed in a certain city a secondary altar with a monumental statue of the Curé d'Ars with a small crucifix four inches high between the boots.

That is why the *Ceremonial of Bishops* adopted the precaution of recommending that this cross should "stand high" and that its base alone should be equal in height to two of the largest candlesticks on the altar. More exact measurements have been given in pontifical directions and for the smallest altars a minimum of one foot has been fixed as the height of the image of the crucifix, not including the base. Besides, the celebrant is instructed to raise his eyes towards the image of our crucified Lord during the holy sacrifice. He can only lower them if the cross is of small proportions and set on the altar itself or, what has actually been observed, if it is laid flat on the altar table.

Its normal place, it is true, is on this table, but on condition that it is tall enough. It may also be on a gradine, in front of the tabernacle—which is inconvenient—or above or, better still, behind, so that the tabernacle may be at the foot of the crucifix and yet not serve as its pedestal. In any case it is certainly in bad taste and a breach of the rule to place the cross in a raised niche or on a throne covered by a baldaquin which is intended solely for the exposition of the Blessed Sacrament. In the latter event the cross should be taken away unless Mass is of necessity celebrated during the exposition: in these circumstances the cross may be put back for the duration of the celebration.

It is obligatory to place the cross in the middle of the altar and it should have the image turned towards the celebrant. It is primarily for him that the cross figures on the altar. If the latter faces the people "in Roman style" it is wrong to attach a crucifix to each side of the cross.

It is permitted to dispense with a cross on the altar if there is a large painted or sculptured crucifix behind it. This exception should not be turned into a rule, for the cross should preserve its traditional form of a movable and not a monumental piece of furniture. It should be made of the same material as that of the candlesticks with which it should stand in line and form an artistic whole. Metal is certainly to be preferred to all other material, iron or bronze for ordinary days, silvered or gilt copper for feast days.

THE PROCESSIONAL CROSS

In addition to the altar cross, which is now a permanent feature, there is the processional or portable cross, used when the altar cross cannot be employed, for processions, the consecration of churches or altars, funeral absolutions, etc. As we have seen, this portable cross is the primitive one, the true liturgical cross.

The name "stational cross" which is still often applied to it indicates its very ancient origin. The *station* was the meeting place of the faithful, who assembled every year on the anniversary of the death of a martyr, on the spot where the latter's tomb was situated. It was also the church (station) in Rome where the pope went in procession for the solemn celebration of the holy mysteries. The cross always headed the procession. The custom therefore seems to date back to the fifth century. For nocturnal processions this cross carried torches or candles on its cross-beams. St John Chrysostom is said to have invented one of this type.

The processional cross, adorned with a crucifix, comprises a staff or shaft and the cross proper. They may be taken apart since the upper portion was placed on the altar. The cross is always supposed to be in sections because the Roman ritual prescribes that the crucifix without a shaft should be used for little children's funerals. According to the authorities this symbolizes the brevity of human life.

For a considerable period it was made of wood, sometimes covered with strips of copper or silver; nowadays it is usually in silver or silvered metal and richly decorated. A spirit of poverty and humility still prompts the use of wooden ones. The main thing is that it should be tall enough to dominate the procession which it leads: Christ himself marches at its head. He who carries it, holding it straight aloft, "heads the procession"; these words of the Ritual mean "heads the clergy". If confraternities, societies or groups of the laity do in fact take part, they march "under their respective banner", but in front of the clergy's cross.

Christ's image is always turned towards the front except in the case of the archiepiscopal cross whose crucifix is turned towards the archbishop who follows it. The clerk, called cross-bearer, who is commissioned to carry it, wears a surplice. He is always bare-headed and never genuflects.

A subdeacon carries the cross in solemn processions, for instance on Candlemas day (February 2nd), when all the clergy, holding candles in their hands, form a procession in memory both of Mary's journey to the temple to present the Infant Jesus, and of the words of the aged Simeon: "Ruler of all, now dost thou let thy servant go in peace, according to thy word; for my own eyes have seen that saving power of thine which thou hast prepared in the sight of all nations" (Luke 2. 29). Likewise for the absolution which follows solemn funeral Masses it is the subdeacon, wearing the vestments of his order and accompanied by two acolytes, who carries the cross and stands at the head of the body.

Since the 1956 reform of the functions of Holy Week, the subdeacon of the Mass is again the cross-bearer for the blessing of the Easter Eve fire, for the procession of light and the chanting of the *Exsultet*. But, in all the other ceremonies of the week—on Palm Sunday, Maundy Thursday, when going to the altar of repose, and on Easter eve, during the blessing of the water and the procession to the baptismal font—it is another subdeacon, if available, who performs this function. In the absence of a subdeacon, an ordinary cleric (and not the subdeacon of the Mass) takes charge of the processional cross.

The chapter cross is that which heads the canons of a cathedral or collegiate chapter when they walk as a body, providing there is at least one celebrant in vestments presiding over the procession.

CHAPTER III

THE SACRED VESSELS

THE CHALICE

The chalice is certainly the most important and most ancient of the sacred vessels used in Catholic liturgy. In early days *chalice* and *cup* were synonymous, namely, one of the vessels used for drinking purposes. They were circular, with a wide opening and usually supplied with short handles and a base.

The chalice plays a very important rôle in Christian worship since we know that Jesus instituted the greatest of the sacraments during the course of a meal. The Gospels and St Paul's First Epistle to the Corinthians when treating of the subject are very reticent concerning the details of this supper which our Saviour shared with his apostles on the eve of his death. According to Jewish computation, it really took place on the same day as his passion since the day began at twilight. Instead of "Maundy Thursday, on the eve of his death", it would be more exact to say "during the first hours of Good Friday, the day of his death".

At that time the Passover was the greatest of the Jewish feasts. Now, we are authoritatively informed about the various phases of this official, traditional and ritual meal as partaken of by Christ's contemporaries. Each guest drank from his own cup, but a communal cup was passed around the table four times as a token of friendship.

Before the meal proper, the head of the family blessed a cup of red wine, which was either undiluted or mixed with water, spiced or mulled, while declaring: "This is the sign of our liberty and the memorial of the flight from Egypt. Blessed be the Lord our God! Blessed be thou, king of the world, who hath created the fruit of the vine!" Then the cup was passed around.

A preliminary dish consisting of bitter herbs, that is, cress, lettuce, parsley, horse-radish, acacia or coriander seeds, was served. These herbs, which grow in abundance in Egypt, were intended to recall the harsh slavery to which the children of Israel were subjected during their exile.

A second cup of wine was passed around. The roast lamb, the principal dish, was then placed on the table together with its traditional sauce, the *charoseth*. This sauce, a kind of thick, highly spiced brew, was a mixture of various fruits, apples, grapes, figs, dates, almonds, nuts, cinnamon, all pounded together and cooked in vinegar. Its brick-red colour recalled the clay which the afflicted Hebrews had formerly moulded for the building of their oppressors' houses.

The family's eldest son, or the youngest of the guests, inquired about the meaning of the feast and the father recounted the ignominies endured in Egypt and the deliverance by which their ancestors escaped from a state of serfdom and regained their freedom. Psalms 112 and 113 were sung. After each half-verse the guests replied, Alleluia (let us praise God).

The real meal did not begin until then. The father of the family took one of the unleavened loaves which stood before him, broke it, blessed and distributed it, saying: "Here is the bread of affliction which our fathers ate during their flight from Egypt. Blessed be thou, Lord, king of the universe, who hast made the wheat spring from the bosom of the earth." This was obviously a fraternal communion rite in the same bread as in the case of the communal cup.

The lamb, cut into pieces, was eaten according to the prescriptions of Mosaic law. It was forbidden to break the bones under penalty of scourging, and what remained over after the meal had to be burned.

The rite of the third cup was the most solemn of all. Each guest held his cup in his hand. The president took the communal cup, which had been refilled, in his two hands, then, holding it in his right hand only, raised it over the table and standing up said the prayer.

This was called "the cup of benediction". When the meal was over, a further cup was poured and sometimes a fifth, and Psalms 119 and 136, that is, the great Hallel, were chanted.

"Into this arrangement our Lord's Last Supper fits very easily", Fr Jungmann, author of the latest work on the Mass, rightly points out.[1] The consecration of the bread is closely linked with the first blessing of the table before the paschal lamb is consumed and perpetuates the rite of the breaking of bread. Instead of following the old Aramean formula "Here is the bread of affliction", Jesus gave it to his apostles, saying, "This is my body, given for you".

The consecration of the chalice is related to the thanksgiving after the meal and revives the custom of the third cup, the "cup of benediction". Christ evidently adapted the formula prescribed for table prayers to his own purposes.

Doubtless the special setting of the paschal feast was not preserved by the disciples, since it could only be used once a year, but the two most solemn phases, in force for all the ritual meals of Friday evening (the beginning of the sabbath), and those of friendly gatherings were retained.

After Pentecost the first Christians revived the Lord's Supper. As they met in the dining-room of some private house they used both the furniture and ordinary vessels which they found there—the chalice was the usual receptacle for drinking. It was made of gold, silver, bronze, tin, lead or even wood but more often of glass.

[1] See *The Mass of the Roman Rite* by J. A. Jungmann, S.J., translated by F. A. Brunner, C.SS.R. New York, Benziger, Vol. I, p. 9.

There is nothing surprising in the fact that the form of the chalice has changed in the course of the centuries. A fourth-century medal certainly gives us its most ancient design—a very slender vessel, resembling the glasses now known as flute glass. Chalices with handles were used for several centuries as is shown on numerous Merovingian coins. They were very probably vessels destined for the distribution of communion to the faithful under the species of wine (ministerial chalices) or to give non-consecrated wine to those who had already communicated (purification chalices).

The semi-oval or conical shape of the primitive cups became hemispherical in Roman times. The massive circular base became larger and flattened at the edge. We have here a real revival of the religious craftwork of the goldsmith. The chalices of the thirteenth century, owing to the symmetry of their form, possess a beauty which will never be surpassed. This Roman shape, with its simple outline, harmonious proportions and discreet decoration, is nowadays the favourite type.

Due to an exaggerated desire for elegance, chalices became taller and taller, copying a wide-open tulip or the graceless shape of an almost cylindrical thimble with raised edges. The base was cut up into leaves covered with enamelled ribbon designs and medallions, the stem and the node were laden with architectural motifs, with buttresses and pinnacles, with loggias and niches and even personages.

A reaction occurred in the last century with the return to medieval art and the hemispherical cup became universal; ornament is rare and of religious inspiration. Nowadays, the metal is bare, hammered or polished, with such possible contrasts as the different materials used in its making allow. The various shades of the gold, silver or patina together with the unadorned catacomb motifs form its sole decoration. We shall never again see chalices in wood, glass, crystal or stone. The Church recommends gold and gilt silver for the cup and permits the use of any other suitable metal for the stem and the base.

When can we see the chalice? It is only used for celebrating Mass and when it is carried it is always covered with a veil. Indeed, at low Mass the priest himself carries it and takes it away concealed in a silken material of the same colour as that worn for the day's Mass.

At high Mass the chalice is prepared on the credence together with the other necessary objects and they are all placed under the large humeral veil which the subdeacon wears over his shoulders at the offertory. The latter carries it to the altar at that moment but it is still concealed by this veil. After the communion the same minister wipes it, furnishes it with the paten and sacred linen, then covers it again with its small veil in order to place it on the credence.

In all, this sacred vessel can only be seen during the middle of the Mass, from the offertory up to the communion inclusive. After the consecration of the wine, the celebrant even shows it to the faithful by raising it above his head. It is then no longer wine but the precious blood of Christ which the congregation is invited to adore.

The chalice is also very much in evidence during ordination ceremonies for major orders. It is carried empty to the bishop so that the subdeacon may touch it with his right hand. It is also presented to the priest on whom the bishop has just imposed his hands, but on this occasion it contains wine and a little water.

THE PATEN

The congregation see even less of the paten. We call it a sacred vessel, in the Latin sense of the word, but it is really a small shallow plate. It, too, is of gold or gilt silver like its corresponding chalice. It holds the altar bread from the beginning of the Mass until the celebrant offers it up and it does not appear again until the moment of communion when it serves as a support for the consecrated host destined for the priest.

At high Mass the subdeacon may be seen to take the paten at the offertory, cover it with the humeral veil and go down the altar steps to stand motionless until the *Pater* is said. This rite calls for some explanation. What is the significance of this action of a minister holding an empty vessel which serves no purpose during the essential part of the holy sacrifice?

We should first of all know that at the time when the faithful themselves brought bread for consecration it was the subdeacons who were entrusted with collecting the offerings in large basins which were called patens. They carried the required amount to the altar and the surplus was kept to supply the needs of the clergy and the poor. The same ministers subsequently wrapped up these patens in the fanons or linen cloths used for wiping them.

At the moment of the communion of the faithful they carried them back to the altar in order to place on them the consecrated bread broken up into pieces. Moreover, the *Sancta* and the *Fermentum* were presented to the pope on patens. This was a wonderful symbol of the unity of the holy sacrifice in time and space. The *Sancta* were fragments of consecrated bread preserved from the preceding papal Mass: this conveyed a striking impression of the unity and the continuity of the same sacrifice. The *Fermentum*, which was also a fragment consecrated in another and sometimes distant church, emphasized the unity of the Church still more explicitly. The pope, or another bishop, had it carried by an acolyte to the celebrant of another Mass to signify that he was "in communion" with him. Both hosts remained on the paten until the *Pax Domini* and were then presented to the celebrant by the subdeacon.

The paten is again used by the deacon of the high Mass when he accompanies the priest during the distribution of communion to the faithful. He places it under each person's chin to catch the host, or fragments of it, should it fall. At low Mass this is replaced by a communion paten. Finally, the celebrant may use it if he has not a ciborium or if he is giving communion to a few people only.

THE CIBORIUM AND ITS DERIVATIVES

The chalice and paten to which we have just referred must be consecrated by the bishop because they are directly used for the holy sacrifice. The ciborium and its derivatives are merely blessed because they are only used to hold consecrated hosts after the Mass.

Indeed, at an early stage, the Church felt it necessary to reserve the Eucharist in order to take it to sick persons and prisoners. This is certainly the origin of the reservation of the Eucharist which parish priests, with a cure of souls, have long been obliged to observe in their churches. One, and only one, tabernacle in each church should be used for the vessels set aside for the Eucharist. They are called ciboriums after the Latin word *cibus*, which means nourishment.

As it is difficult to know before Mass the number of persons who wish to receive communion, ciboriums, which can hold a large number of small hosts, are used. Pius XII however recalled that, when possible, it is proper to consecrate at Mass the altar breads required for the communion of the faithful.

It is useless to seek the word ciborium in the liturgical books; its use there is confined to the stiff baldaquin which covers the altar. The name they apply to the sacred vessels is *pyxides*.

The ancients gave the name pyx (from the Greek *puxis*, box, *puxos*, bush) to little caskets in which jewels were kept. It is very possible that the first Christians, who enjoyed the privilege of taking the Body of Christ into their houses, used these little boxes. This custom lasted until about the fifth century, mainly in the case of monks and hermits who were allowed to give themselves communion owing to the difficulties of communication and distance from churches. This was still tolerated in the east up to the eighth century.

There was no very settled rule affecting the construction of these pyxes. The deacons carried the eucharistic species to the absent and infirm in pyxes of gold, silver, ivory, pottery, wood or even of onyx or jasper which were generally round-shaped but sometimes rectangular or polygonal. They were fastened with a flat lid, with or without hinges, or an arched or conical lid surmounted by a ball or a cross.

It was not unlike the pyx which priests still use today in taking communion to the sick: or they may take the form of little ciboriums with feet or of quite flat pyxes. They are placed in a silken sachet and hung around the neck as the deacons formerly did.

There is another derivative of the ciborium, a real eucharistic pyx, which is used for exposition of the Blessed Sacrament.

The custom of carrying the Blessed Sacrament in procession undoubtedly dates from the middle of the thirteenth century and especially from the institution of the feast of Corpus Christi in 1264. But it would be a mistake to believe that the consecrated host was visible from the beginning; on the contrary, it was carefully concealed in a pyx or better still in a reliquary. It was placed in a crucifix, in the breast of a statue of the risen Christ or of the Blessed Virgin Mary holding the Infant Jesus in her arms, or in a lamb borne by St John the Baptist.

Later small openings furnished with crystal or transparent precious gems allowed the host to be seen. It was then that a special instrument, the lunette or lunar-shaped crescent, was invented. It was made of two metal shields between which a section of the host was inserted so that the major portion of it might be visible to all. It was only then that the term "monstrance" (from *monstrare*, to show) could be employed, a name which was used up to the eighteenth century. We have preserved a large number of them, they are in cathedral treasuries or in museums. The most usual shape employed was the tower, consisting of a vertical cylinder on a jewelled base, decorated with belfries, pinnacles and fortresses and surmounted by a steeple. There were also horizontal cylinders sometimes supported by two angels and surrounded by arched panels depicting the most varied scenes. Monstrances in the form of a sun are more modern; the rays made a timid appearance at first and eventually became the sole, or practically the sole, decoration in the sixteenth century. Two centuries later they were called *ostensorium* which also means to show (*ostendere*).

For some years past, artists have searched for other forms and have reverted to those of the Middle Ages, such as the Blessed Virgin or an angel carrying the lunette. The Church allows them the greatest latitude in this domain, providing always that their work is worthy of him who is shown to the public and that it is surmounted by a cross.

Monstrances are not really sacred vessels since they have no contact with the sacred species. This term should be reserved for the pyx or lunette, which is blessed like the ciborium. The crescent form, moreover, has been replaced by a double circle of gilt silver mounted on a hinge inside which the host is placed. The latter is protected by two crystal disks through which it can be seen.

THE EUCHARISTIC DOVE

For a long time the ciborium and tabernacle were in the graceful form of a dove. It was already in use in the fourth century and some of them were still to be found in the eighteenth. Some are even in use today, at Solesmes, for example, in the choir of the Benedictine abbey, in Paris in the church of Saint-Julien-le-Pauvre, which belongs to the

Greek-Melkite rite (Catholic). The Cistercian abbey of Tamié has recently surrendered the indult authorizing this manner of reserving the Blessed Sacrament.

"For the purpose of sheltering the mystery of love and charity", says Corblet, "it was desired to reproduce the form of the bird which almost all ancient peoples regarded as the symbol of love." Ever since this attractive bird returned to Noah's ark carrying an olive branch in its beak, it has also been regarded as a symbol of reconciliation and peace. This sacred dove, a symbol of the Holy Ghost, who appeared on the banks of the Jordan above our Lord's head while he was being baptized, is also the emblem of the twofold priestly and royal anointing of the Son of God made man. Why should it not also serve as the symbol of sacrifice since the pigeon and the turtle-dove were the only two birds whose sacrifice was permitted by Mosaic Law? It was the holocaust offered by the poor and needy. The dove itself is emblematic of several virtues. It is simple, without cunning or ruse, it represents fraternal charity because it cannot live alone, it is familiar yet prudent.

All the eucharistic doves were in gold, silver or enamelled brass, and rarely in wood or ivory. The sacred species were put inside through a slit made in the back between the two wings and furnished with a hinged lid. A pyx, attached to the dove's beak, was also used. The dove was usually hung on chains from the middle of the baldaquin. In Roman times it rested on a small table, sometimes flanked by low turrets connected by little crenellated walls which formed a kind of fortified enclosure. When the ciborium disappeared a sort of shaft in the form of a crozier was fixed to the reredos of the altar and the pyx was hung from the spiral of this crozier.

In order to protect it from the gaze of the crowd, a movable veil of precious material, supported by a circular metal framework, covered it like a tent. This is clearly the origin of our canopy with which we are nowadays obliged to cover the tabernacle where the sacred species are kept.

Finally, in order to protect them against profanation and irreverence, certain doves were sheltered in a tower which served as a tabernacle. These eucharistic towers may be seen in some old churches in Europe, they are sometimes of stone and hollowed out in a column of the building. They too fell into disuse towards the end of the sixteenth century and only "a centuries old or immemorial custom" sanctions their use. Indeed, the Sacred Congregation of Rites, in a decree dated June 1st, 1957, has "categorically forbidden tabernacles situated outside the altar, for instance, in the walls, on the side or behind the altar or in little constructions or columns separated from the altars".

THE TABERNACLE

This same decree of June 1st, 1957, when treating of certain recent innovations, has given a timely reminder about the rules laid down concerning the placing, security and form of tabernacles.

To begin with, the tabernacle must be on an altar. This is clearly not intended to apply to steel cupboards or safes used to hold the Blessed Sacrament at night. "The tabernacle should normally be placed on the high altar", except in cathedrals, collegiate churches and monasteries where solemn choir offices are chanted, or else in important sanctuaries (places of pilgrimage, churches or chapels visited by tourists, often lacking in reverence), "so that the special devotion of the faithful for some venerated object may not be allowed to overshadow the supreme cult of latria due to the Blessed Sacrament." Besides, Mass is habitually celebrated at the altar where the Holy Eucharist is kept.

As to security, "the tabernacle should be immovably fixed to the altar" so that it cannot be either unscrewed or unsealed. In addition, it "should be strongly closed on all sides and so designed in every respect that all danger of profanation is obviated".

Its shape "should harmonize with the style of the altar

and the church; it should not be too different from those used up to the present. It should not be reduced to a plain box but should, so to speak, represent the real habitation of God among men. It should not be ornamented with unusual symbols or figures which astonish the faithful and which may give rise to wrong interpretations or which have no bearing on the Blessed Sacrament."

Finally, the decree insists on the presence of a conopaeum or tent-like veil and a lamp "during times when the sacred species are kept there". We shall devote considerable space to the lamp. It is not the only or certain sign of the eucharistic presence, since lamps may be lit before all the altars, statues or holy images. Notwithstanding the fact that the tabernacle door may be artistically wrought, the conopaeum, which the church has declared obligatory, is still the sure sign. It should envelop the tabernacle completely, like a tent. We cannot be satisfied with a plain little curtain concealing the front nor with two folds of material raised like theatre curtains and still less with a transparent tissue.

The conopaeum is the tabernacle's real decoration, it is its "garment" which protects it like a kind of loose cover. It should preferably be of silk but any other woollen or linen cloth may be used providing it is worthy of the sacred host. It may be white at all times, because that is the proper colour of the Blessed Sacrament. However, it is more advisable to change its colour every day so that it may synchronize with the feast being celebrated or the liturgical season. Black is the only colour which is not allowed. Violet is used for funeral offices. The interior of the tabernacle should be gilded, but it is sufficient to stretch a precious white-coloured cloth over the sides and the back of the door.

CHAPTER IV

LIGHTING

We are not concerned here with the lighting systems used
in our sanctuaries. It is the business of architects and tech-
nicians to seek the most practical and aesthetical methods
of overcoming darkness. Electricity, in many different
forms, has invaded God's house, and we see no disadvantage in this. Concealed lighting may show to advantage
architectural features, sculptures, works of art and even
the church furniture, but it should at least afford the faithful
the possibility of reading their prayer-books. The Church
allows a wide latitude in this domain providing that we
avoid the practice followed in profane places and amuse-
ment centres and everything redolent of the theatre or
advertisement.

Lights in church have a twofold meaning: a decorative
and a mystic meaning.

When the danger of persecution had passed, Christians
used lamps and candles for religious purposes. In the fifth
century, St Jerome replied to Vigilantius who reproached
them with burning lights in full daylight: "Throughout the
whole of the east candles are lighted to read the Gospel
when the sun is shining: this is done not for the purpose
of overcoming darkness but in order to express our joy."

And the *Ceremonial of Bishops* prescribing the burning
of lamps in churches re-echoes the saint's statement and
indicates the dual reason "as much for worship and decoration as for its mystical significance".

ILLUMINATED CROWNS

Since bonfires have been used from all times to mark occasions of rejoicing, it is quite natural that church lighting should serve the same purpose. Not only does the Church permit it but she particularly recommends it for solemn feast days.

It began with wooden or iron circles hung from chains around the altar or before the "confession" of martyrs. The *Liber Pontificalis* speaks of a a gigantic *pharus* in the form of a cross which could hold up to 3,370 candles.

The emperor Constantine (337) gave 169 lustres supporting 8,730 dolphins, that is, branches shaped like dolphins, for holding lamps and candles, to the basilica of St John Lateran.

During the Romanesque period these crowns of light were divided into several round sections, the whole retaining the general contour of a circle, and with round or square towers situated at the angles.

The largest of the Hildesheim crowns has a circumference of about eighteen yards. It is a copper circle representing a wall, surmounted by silver battlements each of which marks the place for a candle. As in the New Jerusalem of the Apocalypse there are twelve doors each bearing an apostle's name. The whole fortified enclosure is defended by twelve towers bearing the name of the tribes of Israel.

Towards the fifteenth century certain pilgrimage churches adopted the use of pediculate crowns. These crowns, made of red iron, usually circular, occasionally polygonal, comprised superimposed circles of decreasing diameter. The stem which supports them is decorated with knots and based on a tripod.

This type of candelabrum is to be found in almost all French churches; the faithful themselves place on them the little devotional candles which they wish to burn.

Chandeliers, which quickly replaced the hanging crowns, appeared in the sixteenth century. They were loaded with small glass ornaments. Their form has become very banal and too like those which decorate drawing-rooms. Fortu-nately, electricity which now reigns supreme has led to their disappearance.

LAMPS

Oil or wax was formerly used to light the nave and choir of churches. The crowns of light even contained both cups for oil and spikes for candles at the same time. But there have always been lamps, in greater or lesser number, burn-ing in honour of relics and holy images. They are still widely used in the east. In many places in the west their number has decreased and we are often satisfied with the minimum, that is, with the eucharistic lamp which is strictly required. A profusion of lamps is more than lawful and in line with the best tradition. It could not be over encouraged providing that the lamps are effective. The *Ceremonial of Bishops* regulates their use in order to emphasize the importance of the altar and to underline the hierarchical rank of different altars in the same church. Their number should be odd, three at least for the high altar, five at least for the altar where the Blessed Sacrament is kept.

Likewise, one may be placed before side altars as also before the "confession" or *martyrium* where holy relics are kept. They should be lighted on feast-days, at least during Vespers and high Mass.

The regulation calling for at least three lamps before the Blessed Sacrament has fallen into disuse. A single lamp suffices. This is the permanent worship offered to the holy Eucharist, a guard of honour constantly watching, our representative before our Saviour by day and by night. The correct place for this lamp is before the tabernacle, in front of the altar, and it should consequently hang from the vaulting. It should be like a beacon whose light strikes the worshipper's eyes immediately on his entry. It is not normal to put it in a corner or to one side whether or not it is fixed to the wall, nor should it be placed on the credence or the gradines of the altar. The traditional clear glass is preferable for it is the most transparent. However, coloured glasses are not prohibited.

The Church feeds her lamps with olive oil or beeswax which are the purest and most fragrant substances. The oil extracted from olives is the symbol of peace, purity, mildness and strength. In countries where it is not cultivated, another vegetable oil taken from the juice of a fruit or plant, such as linseed, walnut, sesame or colza, may be used. The Holy See leaves it to the discretion of bishops to determine if less expensive mineral oils may be used in poor churches or, as a very last resource, electricity. "Should we thus reckon the cost", said Barbier de Montault, "when the honour of God's house is in question? There are occasions on which economy is sublimely ridiculous."

CANDLESTICKS

Lights in church are not merely fixtures in liturgy. They are also carried during ceremonies and in processions.

This was the original and customary way of honouring high dignitaries. The pagans burned torches in full daylight on emperors' feast-days, as Tertullian remarked. They were also carried in front of Eutropius because of his consular rank. We know that when Antiochus was approaching Jerusalem, Jason and the inhabitants of that city welcomed him magnificently with blazing torches and cheering.

The Church raised no objection to the adoption of this method of honouring its pontiffs. On June 22nd, 431, the bishops assembled for the General Council of Ephesus were surrounded with torches when they left the basilica where they had announced the dogma of Mary's maternity.

According to the oldest *Ordo Romanus*, the pope is accompanied by seven candle-bearers during solemn ceremonies. This custom is still followed at the papal Mass, in the primatial cathedral at Lyons, and in some other churches by permission of the Holy See. This septenary symbol is also employed in the case of higher ministers as of mere acolytes. The number has been reduced to two for bishops and has so continued up to the present day. Later, when it fell to priests themselves to celebrate high Mass, the same honour was conferred upon them.

Thus, whenever the celebrant moves from one place to another, from the sacristy to the altar, or from the altar to the sacristy, he is preceded by two acolytes bearing lighted candles.

In a letter of St Germanus of Paris published by Dom Martène, it is stated that "the deacon who chanted the Gospel was accompanied by seven acolytes each carrying a candle; this was intended to symbolize the seven gifts of the Holy Ghost". We still see the two acolytes preceding the deacon, when he goes to the ambo for the solemn chanting of the Gospel at high Mass. In all processions these same clerics lead the way walking on either side of the processional cross.

The *Roman Pontifical*, referring to the objects to be provided for the consecration of a church, mentions among them two lighted candles, "to be borne in front of the bishop wherever he goes".

Later on, it gives directions for the procession of relics which are carried to the threshold of the church by two priests vested in red chasubles. While two candle-bearers lead the way (being those who accompany the bishop everywhere), some torches should be carried immediately in front of the relic bier, and the pontiff walks at the end of the procession. We have here, then, both the veneration shown to the saints and a mark of reverence for the apostles' successors.

And even the mortal remains of our dead are honoured by the light of candles, of which there are sometimes quite a large number, placed around the catafalque. Their soft mysterious light sheds rays of hope and consolation, of life and joy. Following the example of the early Christians, we, too, carry lighted candles when bearing the bodies of the faithful, destined for future resurrection, to their burial place.

In very early days candlesticks were not allowed on the altar. It was formally forbidden by pontifical rules and provincial councils. On the other hand, iconographic evidence of the Roman period proves that one or several candlesticks were placed on the altar of sacrifice itself, but were removed when the Mass was over. It was not until the thirteenth century that they became permanent fixtures. Was it these that the acolytes carried? There can be no doubt about this. Thus for the pope's Mass, and that of a bishop in his diocese, seven candlesticks should be placed on the altar at which they officiate. The number is reduced to six for all other high Masses. At low Masses two are used or, for bishops, four at the most.

Now that candlesticks have become a permanent feature on altars (some are even placed there which serve no purpose or else there are more than are necessary) two movable ones are reserved for the acolytes who carry them at the head of processions and afterwards place them on the credence or, as is particularly the case during Vespers, on the altar steps. Their base is round for convenient handling. There has been scarcely any change in the shape of ordinary candlesticks, whether of wood, brass, bronze or silver, since the earliest days. They have a base for setting them down, a stem and a candle-ring for collecting the wax droppings. There is usually a spike in the centre of the candle-ring to take candles unless it is hollowed out for pressing them in.

Roman candlesticks are always squat, decorated with

grooves, torsades, and imbricated work intertwined with little sprites. The triangular base is covered with fanciful tracery and rests on three-winged dragon's claws or heads and their bodies form the arrises of the pyramid. The candle-ring consists of a bell-mouthed cup supported by little lizards buttressing the edges.

The general effect of caryatid candlesticks is yet more fantastic: sometimes there is a fabulous bird or a man at grips with a lion supporting the candle-ring and whose bodies form the stem; at other times there is a winged dragon bearing an imp who is thrusting a lance into his jaws.

In the Gothic period the candlesticks grew taller and their stems were covered with numerous and varied chasings or engravings. The fantastic animals were replaced by intertwined vegetation which overran the three lion's paws forming the base, the candle-ring and the knots or knobs, whose numbers increased on account of the height of the stem. In the fifteenth century architectural motifs made their appearance, flamboyant pediments, bell-turrets and platforms.

The Renaissance initiated the mode of exaggerated shapes and dimensions. Some candlesticks even reached a height of six and a half feet. They consisted of a series of balls, spindles and knots threaded on an iron stem which was obviously intended to make it rigid. They were composed of ornamental sunken or round mouldings, narrow channels or spheres, cubes or disks, ornamented with grotesque masks, heads of little winged angels, twisted garlands, the whole designed with artistic delicacy.

During the following centuries candlesticks became monuments exaggeratedly high and being too heavy could not be taken down from the gradines on which they rested. These are the first kinds to have been converted to electricity in certain churches, because neither the sacristan's arm nor even his taper could easily reach them. They became purely ornamental and when the priest came to celebrate Mass nothing more than two little movable candlesticks of a common shape were placed on the altar table. There was an obvious lack of taste here and failure to submit to the most formal of the Church's regulations. The use of electricity is forbidden on the altar itself.

CANDLES

The Church, being faithful to ancient traditions and mindful of symbols which bind the material and the supernatural worlds together, wishes that our candles should be made of beeswax and not of more or less purified animal fat or chemical substances like stearin. The early Fathers praised the purity of wax extracted from the most exquisite juice of flowers by virgin bees. All saw in this an image of Christ's flesh formed from Mary's virginal blood.

The lighted candle represents Jesus, the wick hidden in the wax is the image of his soul, the flame springing from the centre of this waxen column and shining from its summit is the emblem of his divinity. The delicate perfume of this substance represents the fullness of Christ's perfections, *bonus odor Christi*.

The whiteness of the wax is the fruit of much toil, having been worked upon and exposed to the open air and sun, and it also symbolizes the glory of our Saviour's sacred humanity, the result of great labours and sufferings. While it is being slowly consumed beside the cross the candle also reminds us of our Redeemer shedding all his blood drop by drop, for the world's salvation.

The white candles of purified wax are symbols of joy and gladness and suitable for all our Christian feast-days. But the yellow candles, that is, the wax in its raw, unbleached state, are used on days of mourning and penance, on Good Friday, for instance, and at funerals and Masses for the dead.

Since the light of candles beautifies worship and

emphasizes its solemnity the faithful in all countries have a special devotion towards them. They like to take them in their hands, light them and place them near the objects they venerate like relics, holy pictures, statues of saints, tombs, etc. All the crowded sanctuaries, the places of pilgrimage, the localities honoured by an apparition or a miracle furnish ample proof of this age-old custom.

The newly baptized babe receives his candle, as a token of the light which henceforth fills his soul; at her churching, his happy mother comes with another candle in her hand, as a sign of thanksgiving. In the Virgin Mary's time it was a matter of legal purification, which fully justifies the black vestment, symbol of the impurity contracted, worn by the pope in the eighth century, for the feast of February 2nd. The officiant, nowadays too, is vested in a violet cope for the blessing and distribution of candles; but he puts on white vestments for the celebration of Mass, as did the Roman pontiff at Saint Mary Major, to indicate that Mary's purification has been completed. This traditional Candlemas procession, far from being a remnant of paganism as some have wrongly claimed, is merely a representation of the Gospel of the day. Mary carries her child to the Temple. He is "the light of the world". She offers gifts as required by the Law. The candle may aptly serve as the symbol of him. The righteous old man, Simeon, does not hesitate to say to him, "My own eyes have seen that saving power of thine which thou hast prepared in the sight of all the nations".

THE PASCHAL CANDLE

Here is something altogether unique, a liturgical object which is only seen during a period of forty days. It appears at the beginning of the Easter Vigil and is taken away on Ascension Day. We may say that it ceases to exist during the rest of the year; this is the paschal candle, the largest and most venerable of all.

It is said that it was originally intended to give light to the congregation during the long nocturnal office from Holy Saturday to Easter Sunday. The custom of blessing it dates back to the first centuries, but it was reserved to the basilicas and did not spread to the whole Church until after the fifth century.

Since the decree of the Congregation of Rites, of February 9th, 1951, the ceremony of Holy Saturday is no longer celebrated in the morning but compulsorily in the evening, as formerly. The celebrant begins by the blessing of the new fire, at the threshold or outside the church, then he makes incisions in the wax of the large candle with a stylet. He traces a cross between the holes prepared for the grains of incense, then forms the Greek letter *alpha* above the cross, the letter *omega* under the cross and finally the four figures of the date of the current year between the arms of the cross. Since these two letters are the first and last of the Greek alphabet they indicate that Christ is the beginning and end of everything, as the priest says while making the incisions: "Christ, yesterday and today, the beginning of all things and their end, Alpha and Omega, all time belongs to him and all the ages, to him be glory and dominion for all eternity, world without end, Amen."

The deacon then presents five grains of incense to the celebrant which the latter blesses in silence with aspersion and incensing. He then inserts them into the holes prepared in the wax, saying: "By his holy and glorious wounds may Christ the Lord guard and keep us, Amen."

The symbolism of these grains is thus clearly explained; these are the five wounds of the crucified Jesus in which the spices and perfumes, brought to the tomb by Magdalen and her devout companions, are enclosed.

A little candle is lit from the new fire and given by the deacon to the celebrant who lights the wick of the paschal candle. The priest then blesses the candle. The deacon dons the white stole and dalmatic while the thurifer has the incense put in and blessed and then heads the procession.

The church is plunged in darkness. A single flame flickers from the very top of a waxen column and casts its shifting light on those near it. Such is the solemn entry of this majestic candle which represents Christ among us, "the light of the world", "the light which shineth in the darkness", "true light which enlighteneth every man coming into the world", Christ, whose countenance shines in heaven "like the sun in all its splendour". Just as the Hebrews were shown the way on their desert journey by the light of a column of fire, so we too are guided by the light of Truth on the path of salvation. This light dispels our soul's darkness and guides us towards the shining glory of heaven. The deacon who carries the paschal candle is like the harbinger of good news, the angel, ablaze with light, who announced the Master's resurrection to the holy women. He stops three times as does the whole procession, thrice he proclaims *Lumen Christi*, raising the note each time. At the first halt he offers the flame to the celebrant who lights his candle from it; at the second halt, in the middle of the nave, the members of the clergy come to get a light; at the final halt, in the choir before the altar, some of the congregation's candles are lighted and they thus pass on to one another the light from the blessed candle and to all the lights of the church.

At this moment a song of triumph and joy swells forth for the blessing of redemption. The deacon is responsible for this praise of the candle, this solemn eulogy of the light which we know as the *Exsultet* from its opening word. No wonder that the Church took pleasure in embodying in a single piece set to a marvellous melody all the regard which we should have for light, God's creature: "Now let the angelic heavenly choirs exult and let the trumpet of salvation sound the triumph of this mighty King." How great is the dignity of this light destined to brighten the most memorable of nights: "On this night Christ burst the bonds of death and rose victorious from the grave . . . blessed indeed is this, the sole night counted worthy to know the season and the hour in which Christ rose again from the dead. . . . The night on which heaven is wedded to earth, the things of God to those of man."

When this, the *Praeconium paschale*, is over, the deacon takes off the white vestments, the congregation put out their candles and sit down and the subdeacon puts the processional cross back in its place. Before the celebration of Mass a server carries the paschal candle on its candle-stick to a place near the altar. It will remain there until the feast of the Ascension, when, after the singing of the Gos-pel, it is put out. After Mass it is finally removed from the choir.

The gigantic candlestick sometimes as high as nine or twelve feet, which our forefathers used to cover with gold, silver or ivory and always decorated artistically, was used as the paschal candlestick, proportionate in size to the very large candle it is intended to support; it is the trophy of the cross, the trunk of that mystical tree on which our Saviour died. Of late years an attempt has been made to revive the custom of attaching a paschal table or chart to the candle. This is a simple sheet of vellum showing the year since creation, the Incarnation, the founding of the church where the candle stands, the year of the reigning pontiff and sovereign, the epact, the golden number, the dominical letter together with all the movable feasts from Easter to Easter.

CHAPTER V

THE LITURGICAL BOOKS

The ark which contains the Torah is found at the far end
of all synagogues in a kind of sanctuary. The Torah is
essentially the whole of the five books of Moses (the
Pentateuch) to which are added the prophetic and hagio-
graphical writings of the Old Testament. The leather or
parchment scrolls contained in the ark are rightly venerated
and treated as persons. The ends of the batons on which
they are rolled up are ornamented with pomegranates and
bell-shaped flowers and surmounted by a crown. Each
volume is wrapped up in a kind of richly embroidered
silken or velvet robe. A perpetual lamp, which is often
surrounded by other lights, burns before the ark which is
veiled by a tapestry. The ark is opened when certain inter-
cessory prayers of especial solemnity are being said, as if
to gain direct access to the divinity.

There is also a kind of casket in our Catholic churches
but it does not hold the holy Scriptures. Although we too,
like the Jews, have a great reverence for the Bible, the sole
authentic word of God, our casket, which we call "tabernacle", holds far more. We believe in the real presence of
our Lord Jesus Christ, hidden under the eucharistic species.
The tabernacle also is veiled and is carefully locked, with
a lamp burning perpetually before it. That is the main
reason why we cannot see the Book of Books in our
churches: the Word of God yields pride of place to God
himself.

It must not be concluded that this unique book, this liturgical book, is not there at all. Although it is not lying on an altar or on a stand, nor kept in a cupboard in the sacristy, it is present everywhere, in daily use, and forms the texture of all the offices and the basis of all the liturgical books. Holy Scripture is read every day, sung at every moment and has inspired all the texts of the Missal, the Breviary, Ritual and Pontifical.

THE READING OF THE BIBLE

In the first place, Christians, like the Jews, read some of the Bible every day. The tradition of the synagogues has been perfectly observed; the first Christians continued to do what St Paul and his companions had noticed amongst the Jews at Pisidia: "They went and took their seats in the synagogue on the Sabbath day. When the reading from the law and the prophets was finished, the rulers of the synagogue sent a message to them to say, Brethren, if you have in your hearts any word of encouragement for the people, let us hear it" (Acts 13. 14).

To this the Christians added the reading of the apostles' Epistles (as St Paul had advised the Colossians and Laodiceans to do), and later on that of the Gospels. This is what we find in the Missal with the one difference that the books of the Old Testament are rarely used.

In the beginning the text was read by a deacon or a reader from a complete manuscript on which the opening and end of the readings were marked according to the orders given by the bishop, or else the latter made a sign to stop when he wished. In the sixth century the Epistles were already partly divided up as they are today and these selected pieces were gradually collected into a volume which was called the *Epistolarium*. The same was done with the Gospel passages chosen for reading in the first part of the Mass. This collection became the *Evangelarium* for the use of the deacon whose duty it was to chant the Gospel of the day.

Our present Missal, therefore, contains the "pericopes" for each Mass, that is, the passages appointed for reading together with the texts reserved to the celebrant which formerly comprised a separate volume, the Sacramentary. Even the words (without music) for the different parts which should be sung by the choir are added; they are collected together, with music, in a book called the Gradual. Thus, the priest who is celebrating a private Mass can have at hand all the texts which in the case of high Mass are assigned to the subdeacon, the deacon and the choir.

Our present-day Breviary follows the same pattern. The passages of the Bible chosen for the night office were first collected together. A passage from the Old or New Testament is still appointed for each day in the office called Matins which is nowadays said by monks and nuns during the night or at dawn. Thus the greater portion of the Bible is read either in the monastery choir or privately by priests and certain religious communities: Genesis during Septuagesima; the prophetic writings during penitential seasons such as Advent and Lent; the Acts of the Apostles after Easter; the books of Kings after Pentecost; the books of Wisdom in August; the little monographs of Job, Tobias, Judith and Esther in September; the Machabees in October, etc.

THE MARTYROLOGY

At the office of Prime, that is, at sunrise, choir religious use a book which is very different from all the others: it contains no biblical text. It is the official list of the saints honoured by the Church. Its name obviously derives from the martyrs who were the first to be the object of special veneration and, as a general rule, on the anniversary of their death. The first Christians called it the day of their heavenly birthday (*natalis dies* or simply *natalis*).

Lists were drawn up from a very early date in the

Christian churches and were jealously preserved. At Hippo, for instance, the account of their passion and death was read during the office. Almost everywhere their names were mentioned during the canon of the Mass. Ivory or wooden tablets coated in wax on which writing was engraved with a stylet were used for this purpose. They were called diptychs (to bend in two) and were coupled together with a hinge and folded back on each other, thus protecting the wax. Authentic traces of this practice are preserved in the Roman Missal. When the celebrant has prayed for the Church and her living members he says the *Communicantes* and after the elevation the *Nobis quoque*, which are simply two diptychs of early Christian days. The apostles are mentioned in them, then the first popes and some martyrs. As this enumeration of holy personages grew constantly longer the list had to be settled once and for all.

Today, when the sovereign pontiff canonizes a saint (which meant originally putting him in the canon of the Mass) his name is placed in the Martyrology with a brief eulogy and very summary biographical notes. In contrast with all the other liturgical books, this catalogue of saints begins on January 1st, like the civil calendar, instead of on the first Sunday in Advent.

In monasteries, at the time of Prime, after the psalms, the Little Chapter and collect, the monks go to the chapter house and a lector reads the passage of the Martyrology containing the names of the following day's saints. In cathedral or collegiate churches, where the whole office is sung in choir, the lector goes to the lectern for this reading.

THE PONTIFICAL

The ceremonial for bishops is slightly different from that for priests. Not only do they wear certain insignia specially reserved to them, but they are assisted by a greater number of sacred and lesser ministers. Thus, a bishop may not celebrate the ordinary high Mass, he may only sing the pontifical Mass.

In addition to the usual deacon and subdeacon the prelate is assisted by a priest wearing a cope and, if he is in his own diocese, two other deacons take their places by the sides of his throne. It is obvious that very exact rules must be made for this special ceremonial and that each officiating minister must understand the functions which he has to fulfil during the celebration.

These rules are contained in two liturgical books, the *Ceremonial of Bishops* and the *Roman Pontifical*.

The *Ceremonial of Bishops* describes in minute detail the ceremonies of Mass and the Office, when the bishop himself is celebrating or when he attends them in his pontifical capacity. The first part sets out the general principles to be followed in all pontifical functions, from the election of a bishop and his entry into his diocese, his liturgical responsibilities, duties and privileges, down to his last illness, death and funeral. All who assist the bishop, both priests and clerics, will find in this book and in no other the description of their office and the rites, such as bowings, kissings, incensings, etc., they have to perform. Besides the celebration of Mass and divine Office the second part of the *Ceremonial* gives the special features proper to certain days of the Christian year from Advent to Corpus Christi.

The second liturgical book for bishops is the Roman Pontifical, which contains all the functions reserved to them, excluding Mass and the Office. It should be noted that the bishop administers most of the sacraments in the same way as priests. This is so for the Eucharist, penance and extreme unction. He may also confer baptism and celebrate marriage without any special solemnity. It is more normal that he should do so with the insignia of his rank, that is with his mitre and his crozier, having first put on his cope. But the Pontifical begins by describing the two sacraments, confirmation and holy orders, which are habitually administered by him.

The bishop's first responsibility is to communicate

Christ's priesthood which he possesses to a full and super-abundant degree, for it is his main preoccupation to have priests, holy priests, who can minister on his behalf to the faithful whom he cannot personally reach. The detailed description of ordinations is followed by more exceptional ceremonies: the consecration of a bishop which is, so to speak, the climax; the conferring of the pallium on an archbishop; the blessing of abbots and abbesses; the consecration of virgins; the crowning of kings and queens and finally the blessing of knights.

After persons come things. Firstly sacred places, beginning with the blessing and laying of the foundation stone of a public church or chapel.

A considerable portion of the Pontifical is devoted to the dedication or consecration of a church for it is certainly the most important of all liturgical functions both as regards the number of rites and the length of time it takes. To these are added the consecration of a permanent altar as distinct from that of the church which contains it; the consecration of movable altars, which we usually call "altar stones" and which are really small-sized altars which may be taken from place to place. The important series of sacred places concludes with the blessing of cemeteries and their re-dedication in the case of profanation.

The objects whose blessing is reserved to the bishop are: chalices, patens and other sacred vessels; liturgical vestments, cloths and corporals; crosses, images of saints, reliquaries and bells. That does not mean that some of them, such as the liturgical vestments and cloths, may not be blessed by a priest acting as his bishop's delegate. Finally, the last part of the Pontifical includes the celebration of several feasts and certain occasional functions like the announcement of movable feasts made to a solemn chant in cathedrals at the Epiphany.

After the Gospel of the Mass, the assistant priest or the canon charged with this duty, vested in a white cope, goes

to the lectern, which is adorned with white silk, and sings
in Latin: "Know, beloved brethren, that by God's mercy,
as we have rejoiced in the nativity of our Lord Jesus
Christ, so also we proclaim to you today the coming joys
of the resurrection of this same God and Saviour. On ——
will be Septuagesima Sunday, the —— will be Ash Wednesday and the beginning of the Lenten fast. The ——
(March or April) you will joyously celebrate the holy Pasch
of our Lord Jesus Christ; . . . The —— (November or
December) will be the first Sunday in Advent of Our Lord
Jesus Christ, to whom be honour and glory for ever and
ever Amen."

The Pontifical, after this solemn introduction to the
liturgical year, gives us two ceremonies which have fallen
into disuse, but which are rich in history and doctrine, the
expulsion of penitents, fixed for Ash Wednesday, and their
reconciliation which took place on Maundy Thursday.
Three Masses were formerly celebrated on that day: the
penitents' Mass has long since ceased, that of the consecration of the Holy Oils combined with that of the com-
memoration of the Eucharist was separated from it in 1956
and, under the name of Mass of the Chrism, is now only
celebrated in his cathedral by the bishop. The third Mass,
at which all the faithful are invited to receive communion,
in remembrance of our Lord's last Supper, is now said in
the evening, at supper-time.

The Pontifical finally describes the ceremonial for synods
or periodical ecclesiastical meetings; the visitation of
parishes which the bishop carries out regularly in his
diocese; the reception of civil authorities in churches, etc.

CHAPTER VI

THE THURIBLE

The thurible used in Catholic churches is composed of a little metal bowl hanging from three chains and holding burning charcoal. It is a perfume burner in which the grains of incense are slowly consumed and give off a sweet-smelling smoke. Incense is an oriental product. Orientals are fond of perfumes. This, however, does not warrant the assumption made by de Vert that the object of incensing is to drive away bad smells. Incense and other resins or fragrant plants have been burned in honour of the divinity in all ages. Among the peoples of pagan antiquity incense was already reserved for religious purposes and every offering made to the gods was accompanied by the burning of incense. It was not merely the gift of a precious object, but a true sacrifice since this matter was consumed, like a victim, in the divinity's presence.

Thousands of years ago the Egyptians were familiar with this indispensable element of worship, when the Jewish people were taking form in their country. Indeed, the Egyptian funeral had long since taken on a pomp which made it all at once like a procession, a removal and a crossing. The sarcophagus laid beneath a catafalque was placed on top of a ceremonial barque. This was supported on a sledge drawn by a team of oxen. A priest whose shoulders were covered by the skin of a panther went before it burning incense. When the Nile was crossed, the oxen were unharnessed and the men drew or carried the catafalque, "preceded by a priest who continually sprinkled it with water and held a burning thurible at arm's length in its direction" (P. Montet, *La vie quotidienne en Egypte*).

Inside the closed and dim temples, the priest incensed the god's or goddess's statue of gilt wood. On certain feasts one or other of these statues was borne in procession and at least one and sometimes several priests, clothed in panther skins, walked before it burning incense in a thurible at the end of a handle. The Egyptian thuribles, in fact, were in the form of a metal hand and an arm which served as a handle. A small vessel in the hand held the charcoal. Midway up the arm another little receptacle contained the incense. The article was held in the left hand and the right hand was used for sprinkling incense on the burning charcoal. The smoking thurible was then presented to the divinity in order that he might, so to speak, breathe in the odour which came from it. This act of offering clearly explains the gentle swing that the thurifer gives his thurible. "To give a swing of the thurible" is in fact to cast the incense-burner in the direction of the person or object to be incensed.

This is perhaps not an altogether correct expression. "The thurible is not swung", writes M. Paul Bayart in *Liturgia*, "despite the poets, neither is it cast. It is presented by lifting it up and sending it gently towards the person or thing which we wish to honour."

This is very true as regards persons, but we shall see later that for processions the thurible must really be kept continually swinging for the purpose of incensing the whole procession. And it is also necessary to swing the thurible when it is not in use during ceremonies, otherwise there is some danger that the charcoal will go out. Since men deem it a great honour to offer a person pleasant vapours to inhale, God, who deigns to act in a human manner with men, willed that the vapour of incense should be used in the rites of his worship. Do we not endow him with eyes to see our hands joined in supplication, ears to hear the prayers offered by our lips? Why should we not rightly assume that God is pleased with a sweet-smelling substance? May we not think that God looks with pleasure on the fragrant clouds pouring from the burning charcoal and going up towards him?

The white wreaths of smoke which come from this vessel and rise towards heaven are in fact a symbol of our prayer which ascends from the earth towards the dwelling of the All-Highest. King David said in a psalm: "May my prayer rise towards you, Lord, like incense smoke."

In the time of Moses the Jewish priests used a perfume made up of equal parts of spices, of stacte, onyx, galbanum and incense. In the temple of Jerusalem a combination of thirteen different perfumes was burned on an altar specially reserved for this rite and which was known as the altar of incense. This little piece of furniture was square and made of acacia wood covered with strips of gold; it was about three feet high and a foot and a half wide. Morning and night, after the ritual slaughtering of a lamb and its quartering, the priests, chosen by lot to burn the incense, took burning charcoal from the principal altar of sacrifices in the court, and then entered the "Holy of Holies" successively to perform their office.

The first placed the charcoals on the altar of incense and withdrew. Another poured a fixed amount of incense, handed the receptacle for spices back to the levite who was assisting him and remained alone for some moments in prayer. During the burning of the victim which followed, cakes were offered and a libation of wine poured out. Finally, but only at the morning ceremony, the priest who had burned the incense went with the other priests as far as the dais and blessed the people from there. The formula dated back to Moses himself: "The Lord bless thee, and keep thee; the Lord smile on thee, and be merciful to thee; the Lord turn his regard towards thee, and give thee peace" (Numb. 6. 24–6).

The Romans, too, used incense in their worship and that is why the first Christians did not make use of it during the three centuries of persecution. At first, since they were obliged to celebrate their offices in secret, the use of such a clinging perfume would have betrayed them. Besides, this practice evoked too many pagan memories. And they were very tragic memories—when a Christian was denounced and appeared before the judges, they began by promising him his freedom if he apostatized. There was always a little pagan altar with a *batillum* in the court of justice. The *batillum* was a rectangular brazier in bronze, copper or gold, sometimes even a plain little shovel which contained slowly burning embers. In order to show one's adherence to the worship of idols it was enough to throw a pinch of incense on the burning charcoal. Good Christians preferred to surrender their bodies to the executioners in order to save their souls.[1] When the governor of a town wished to know if there were any Christians among the inhabitants, he had merely to organize a public ceremony and oblige the whole population to offer a little incense before the emperor's statue. Those who hid themselves or attempted to flee were inevitably condemned.

But, in the fourth century, when the Church had triumphed over her persecutors and when Christianity was officially recognized and churches could be built and the holy sacrifice of the Mass openly celebrated, the disciples of Christ then began using incense for their ceremonies.

Doubtless the orientals still used thuribles with handles and without a lid, but the covered spherical incense burner hanging on one or three chains came quickly into general use. In order to lay it down easily a foot was added, very low and in circular or tripod form, the cover was then furnished with a ring or a ball, before taking on the varied shapes of the Middle Ages; a tower, a little lantern, a campanile, a fortress, etc.

[1] "If the offering of incense honours God, to offer it to idols is a sign of idolatry" (1 Mach. 1. 58).

In the Gothic period, the foot, cup and lid grew taller and had numerous sides ornamented with foliage or animals. Religious motifs were often even carved or sculptured upon them, such as Christ, our Lady, the apostles and angels and sometimes coats of arms. With the Renaissance the cup and lid became convex and then grew disproportionately long. In the nineteenth century, the thurible finally inherited all the faults of the other periods without having any of their qualities. At the moment it has taken on simpler shapes, nearly always spherical with an unadorned lid which slips along the three chains and which may be raised as required on a fourth chain.

All non-fusible metals are used in making it, iron, copper and bronze. Our forefathers' silver and gold have been replaced by imitation bronze, silvered or gilt.

The largest thurible in the world is in Spain. It is as tall as a man and hangs from four quite short chains. It may be seen in the sacristy of Saint James of Compostella. For great feast-days and exceptional occasions, filled with burning charcoal, it is hung on a cable which is itself attached to a windlass. Worked by eight sturdy policemen dressed in red the *botafumeiro* swings under the dome, at the intersection of the transept. It was used in January 1956 in honour of the English Admiral Briggs, who made a solemn presentation of a British flag to the apostle St James, patron of all Spain.

When and how is the thurible used in the ceremonies of Catholic worship? For all solemn functions a cleric is appointed to carry the thurible, keep the charcoal burning, hand it to the officiant for the imposition and blessing of the incense and, finally, to give it to the person who is to do the censing, if he himself is not doing so. The use of the thurible is prescribed for all Masses with the exception of low Masses, for the principal Hours of the divine Office, that is, Lauds and Vespers, expositions, benedictions and repositions of the Blessed Sacrament, for almost all processions, for ordinations and consecrations of bishops, for the reception of prelates, for the consecration of churches and altars, etc.

There is an admirable scale fixed for the liturgical honours to be conferred on different persons, whether ecclesiastical or secular, by means of censings. Firstly there is the choice of the thurifer. At high Mass it is the deacon who censes the priests while it is an ordinary cleric who censes the lesser ministers and the congregation. In cathedrals a deacon canon censes his colleagues in the chapter, a cleric then takes the censer and censes the priests, the acolytes and the congregation.

This scale also covers the place which each person occupies in the office which is being celebrated. Thus it is easy to recognize the hierarchy of what we may term honour, superimposed on the hierarchy of rank, though they are not in conflict. The highest censing is comprised of three double swings, that is, the thurible is swung three times before the person. This censing is done kneeling for the Blessed Sacrament and standing for all the persons or things which represent our Lord Jesus Christ. Thus the pope, who remains seated, is censed by a dignitary of the pontifical court.

The thurifer remains standing when censing other persons: a cardinal, a legate, the archbishop in his province, the bishop in his diocese. All bishops are censed in the same way, except when the diocesan bishop or a higher prelate is present at the throne. Finally, the celebrant of the Mass, except in the last mentioned case, is also censed with three double swings, because he too represents our Lord, even were he only twenty-four years old and ordained the previous day.

On what things is a similar honour conferred? The crucifix or an ordinary cross, such as are engraved on the walls of consecrated churches; a relic of the true cross and even other relics of the passion, such as the holy crown of thorns, the nails and the winding-sheet; a statue or picture of the Divine Persons. The Gospel book and the Missal, because they contain the Word of God, are equally honoured.

The second category of censings consists of only two double swings. It is given to all prelates who are not bishops, to vicars-general or vicars capitular, to mitred abbots, to superior-generals of orders and to the superior or rector of the church where the office is being celebrated. All vested ministers are given this same censing; the deacon and subdeacon, the cantors, the assistant priest and the two deacons at the throne at pontifical Mass.

Ordinary priests are censed with one double swing and they are even included collectively if there is a large number of them. It should be noted, in order to end this rather long list, that all those who are not priests, such as seminarists, servers, lower ministers and the faithful, are censed with single swings. The thurifer does not raise the censer so high and lowers it immediately. This way of censing is suited to the altar, to bread and wine presented at the offertory, to the catafalque set up for funeral offices, finally to objects which receive a blessing, such as candles, ashes and palms.

The perfume of the incense which has been blessed beforehand is mainly meant to sanctify persons and things rather than to honour them. Besides, the homage belongs to God himself who lives in the souls regenerated by baptism. It must not be forgotten that incense is consumed in honour of the divinity.

The thurible is also used in processions but in this case it is a matter of continual incensing of whatever is particularly honoured on that day. Thus the thurifer, with his smoking thurible, takes up different positions according to the nature of the procession. He nearly always walks in front, before the processional cross: he thus honours the image of our crucified Lord and, in addition, the smoke perfumes the whole procession.

If a relic or a statue is carried the cleric in charge of the thurible walks before the bearers, which clearly shows that he wishes to honour the mortal remains of the saints or their image; this is a relative veneration which is really addressed to the persons who are enjoying the beatific vision in heaven. Did not the ancients use incense for victories? There can be no greater triumph than that of the Blessed Sacrament which we celebrate in Corpus Christi processions. Then there are two thurifers, walking side by side, who go in front of the canopy beneath which the golden monstrance is carried: they swing their smoking thuribles continuously. The only other occasion on which this ceremonial occurs is on Maundy Thursday, when, at the conclusion of Mass, the celebrant solemnly bears the ciborium to the altar of repose. Before leaving the high altar, and when reaching the chapel adorned in white decorated with flowers and an imposing array of candles, the priest holds the thurible in his hands and, kneeling down, offers the highest honours to the Holy Eucharist.

CHAPTER VII

THE FONT

Water plays an important part in man's life. It is the indispensable setting for all life's phenomena, and the fruitful origin of all things: it nourishes the earth and all its inhabitants, men, animals and plants. It refreshes and invigorates but it also washes and purifies. It is this latter property which religions have chiefly exploited by making use of water as a symbol of moral purification.

Firstly, legal purification, which does not necessarily imply a sincere regret for sins which have been committed. We are told that the ancient pagans never entered their temples without purifying themselves with lustral water. Vessels called *aquæ minaria*, full of this water, were placed in the entrance hall of the places of worship. When coming out of them the believers took some of it away with them to use in their dwellings. No sacrifice was offered until the people had first been purified with the water of atonement. The Romans had such great respect for this water that if it fell on the ground, or even if the vessels containing it were put on the ground, during their sacrifices, they considered this a sacrilege and an evil augury. That is why they invented an earthen vessel called *Futile*, very wide at the mouth and very narrow at the base, so that it could not stand upright but had to be carried between the hands. This was the duty of young girls and boys, the *camilli*, who wore crowns and were the servants of the Flamines and the Vestals.

As trustees of divine power, the patriarchs, Moses, the synagogue and the prophets prepared blessed water and used it for the purification and deliverance of men and creatures. It is difficult to find a single ceremony in the Old Covenant in which water is not used. Moses, when he had come down from the mountain with the two Tables of the Law, prepared blessed water which he mixed with the blood of victims to sprinkle Israel. The Mosaic prescriptions constantly refer to its use. For persons who were afflicted with leprosy; for persons who had carried the bodies of certain animals; for those who had eaten their flesh; those who had incurred some legal stain were ordered to purify themselves with water. Moreover, a large and magnificent metal basin was placed in the court of the Temple. It was filled with clear water and called the sea of brass. The members of twenty-four sacerdotal families washed themselves in it before commencing their daily functions. The faithful also washed their hands and their heads before crossing the threshold of the sanctuary and even before their private prayers.

We find the same law amongst the Moslems. Even today there are tanks or fountains at the doors of mosques, usually in an inner court, in which they never fail to wash themselves before praying. "In order to be valid", writes Fr J. M. Abd-el-Jalib, "the ritual prayer must be preceded by ablutions. For complete ablutions the whole body must be washed. For partial ablutions it is enough to pour a little water on the hands, into the mouth, the nostrils, on the front of the face, on the forearms, on the scalp, on the ears, on the nape of the neck and on the feet." Before beginning, the believer turns towards Mecca and says: "In the name of Allah, the clement, the merciful, my God, I fly to thee for refuge against the barbs of the demons, and I fly to thee that thou mayest save me from their presence." The separate actions of washing are accompanied by certain formulas. All pious Moslems know them by heart.

From the beginning the Church has made use of this mighty symbol of water after the example of her divine Founder who wished to be baptized in the Jordan by John and who gave explicit orders to his disciples to baptize all those who believe "In the name of the Father and of the Son and of the Holy Ghost". The blessed water of the Old Covenant washed away breaches of the law, the holy water of the New Law washes away the stains of the soul, the gravest sins in the case of the adult who receives baptism, venial sins in the case of a person using ordinary holy water.

Indeed, there are three kinds of holy water in Catholic liturgy: ordinary holy water, which we find at the entrances of all our churches and chapels; baptismal water, which is reserved for the sacrament of baptism; lastly, Gregorian water, whose use is confined to the consecration of churches and altars.

They differ from each other either by the nature of the elements of which they are composed or by the special blessings given to each or according to the purpose for which they are intended. It is curious to note that the first of these holy waters comprises two elements only (water and salt), and the second three elements (water, the oil of catechumens and holy chrism) and the third of four elements (water, salt, ashes and wine).

ORDINARY HOLY WATER

The twofold purpose of ordinary holy water is to purify and protect: to purify man from the stains of venial sin and to protect him against diabolical temptations. To purify all creatures from the evil influences of the devil and to protect them against everything which threatens their life, health and possessions. This double function of holy water is clearly expressed in the magnificent exorcisms and the prayers, the formulas which sanctify it.

To bless water means in the first place to conjure Satan

(*exorcism* signifies "command") to leave the creature which is dedicated to God, and then to endow it with a virtue which is not inherent in its substance, and which makes it apt to produce effects, supernatural effects, which are beyond its nature.

The *cantharus*, a basin hollowed out in the middle of the atrium of private houses and primitive basilicas, is very probably the forerunner of our fixed stoups. The Christians of the first centuries washed their hands and face in it before entering the sacred enclosure. This custom fell into disuse because of its inconvenience and of the confined space of the atriums which became overcrowded: the faithful were consequently satisfied with a symbolical ablution. Small portable buckets were placed at the entrance of churches or before the piers of the main door on brackets or little tables. The faithful merely dipped the tips of their fingers into the water while saying a prayer or making the sign of the cross. Boldetti, J. B. de Rossi and other archaeologists who explored the catacombs before they were stripped of so many precious souvenirs, stated that they came across spherical shells and little vessels in marble or baked earthenware placed on columns like our modern stoups. The latter came into being about the eleventh or twelfth century. They are often shaped like capitals, the higher portion of which is hollowed out, or like little stone basins laid on massive supports.

Viollet-le-Duc has remarked that "the thirteenth-century architects liked to incorporate all the necessary accessories in the buildings". Thus the stoups provided for in church buildings were no longer furniture but objects which were an integral part of the architecture. They were usually polygonal basins, supported by the frustrum of a little column or some sort of base, whence their name of *pediculate* font. In the Gothic period these little basins went with decorative motifs and wrought dais. "Sometimes", says the same writer, "the sculptors were seized with a fancy to represent serpents, frogs and fish at the bottom of the stoups. Such childishness was in quite bad taste but many people admire them. If these frivolities were intended to remind the faithful that they should take holy water on entering the church it must be admitted that this rather odd way of drawing attention was very successful."

The Renaissance has left us very rich marble stoups, supported by personages. They were often placed outside the door, at least in monasteries, and not inside and this would seem to be the proper place to put them.

Stoups which are made in our day are frequently inserted in the walls, beside the doors, of our modern churches and chapels, and are often placed on both the right and the left of the entrance. They are made of stone, cement or mosaic and shaped like basins or shells. On entering the church all the faithful bless themselves with the water they contain and some, though this is not very logical, even use it on leaving. Who would dream of wiping his feet on leaving the house?

PORTABLE CONTAINERS

Little buckets made of bronze, lead or earthenware containing ordinary holy water were used in the Church from an early date. The term "water for aspersion" has been used for a long time in order to distinguish this water from baptismal water. And it fully explains the purpose for which it was used at all periods. In our day these containers are silvered, or sometimes gilt copper, furnished with a handle which makes them easy to carry. They always have a sprinkler at the end of whose wooden handle there is a perforated ball which holds the water for aspersion.

The practice of sprinkling at Sunday high Mass dates back at least to Hincmar of Rheims (806–82). We give here a translation of a passage from one of his synodal letters: "Every Sunday before high Mass each priest should proceed to bless water in a clean vessel worthy of its lofty purpose; he should sprinkle the people who enter the church; those who wish to do so may take some of this water away in clean vessels and sprinkle their fields, their vines, their tables and even their food and drink."

Since the faithful are recommended to keep holy water in their homes they usually have domestic stoups which could be modelled to great advantage on the shapes of liturgical holy water containers.

BAPTISMAL WATER

Since 1956 the parish priest prepares the water for baptism for the year only once annually. This is done on Easter eve in the presence of a gathering of the faithful. According to the new *Ordo* of Holy Week a fairly large vessel must be used which is placed in the middle of the choir and then carried in procession to the baptismal font.

The receptacle reserved for this water which has been the object of the greatest veneration down through the Christian ages is another vessel, fixed and even sealed in a special part of the church which is often called the chapel of the font. The superb baptisteries of Pisa, Florence and Rome were built for it together with other masterpieces of art whose magnificence believers justified by inscribing in large golden letters, engraved on the facing of these monuments: *We are reborn here to immortality.* These vessels cannot be properly called stoups but they are receptacles which closely resemble our fixed stoups although they have a greater capacity. We should at least mention them as absolutely essential furnishings in parish churches.

Although in the early ages of the Christian era people were baptized in rivers, lakes and ponds, large vessels filled with water were also used into which the candidates for baptism entered; they were immersed up to the knees at least. When baptism by infusion became the general method in the west these receptacles grew smaller and were raised up from the ground in order that the neophyte's head could be conveniently held over them.

GREGORIAN WATER

The third kind of holy water is specially reserved for churches and altars. After the rites in preparation for their consecration have been performed, the bishop goes to the credence where the elements which make up this water are ready. He is first of all handed the salt which he exorcizes and blesses. Salt is the origin of health and fertility; when used as a condiment it flavours and preserves. The Jews never offered an unsalted victim and our Lord himself recommends us to use salt in social relations and to look upon it as a symbol of concord and peace. He wishes his apostles to be the salt of the earth, that is, that their speech should not be insipid but that it should incite and urge its hearers towards goodness and induce them to practise virtue.

The consecrator does the same with the water which is handed to him in a suitable container. This usually consists of a glass bowl large enough to hold all the water necessary for the sprinkling of the altar and the church and, if need be, for that of the side altars which are consecrated during the same ceremony.

Ashes, with which the Jews sprinkled their heads so often, through humility and a spirit of penance, obviously symbolize the feelings of compunction and true contrition which should fill our hearts. In this case they signify still more: not alone an ordinary man's or people's humility but that of the Man-God who represents the whole of humanity. This was a sanctifying and atoning humility which he practised to the point of self-annihilation. The bishop blesses these ashes and mixes them with the salt. He then drops this mixture of salt and ashes into the water three times, making the sign of the cross on each occasion.

Finally, a cruet of wine is given to the bishop. He blesses this last element, a symbol of spiritual abundance, of strength, life and joy, and then pours it into the vessel described above.

The name, Gregorian water, it should be noted, is not primitive. It is the Christian name for the lustral water of the pagans who drew a glowing coal from the hearth of the gods and extinguished it by plunging it into the water. By analogy this term of lustral water was used up to the time of the directions given by St Gregory (590–604). In fact on July 18th, 601, he wrote to St Mellitus, one of the missionaries in England: "In order to consecrate for worship the pagan temples turned into churches they must be sprinkled with lustral water and an altar must be raised and the relics placed in it."

CHAPTER VIII

VESSELS FOR HOLY OILS AND OTHER THINGS

It would appear that there were originally no special receptacles for keeping the holy oils. Chrismal patens are the only things which seem to have been used for anointings. We must distinguish between the vessels, the large *ampullae* which are meant for keeping the diocesan supplies of the oils, the smaller containers for the supply of each parish or church, and the small "stocks" with a large opening through which the bishop or priest moistens his thumb for ritual unctions.

In the twelfth and thirteenth centuries the larger containers were called "chrismers", "Chrismals" or pyxes. They usually had a little silver spoon or *spatula* to dispense the oil. Some have been preserved which are shaped like a tower surmounted by a conical roof or belfry. The custom arose of putting the three oils which the Church used then as now in three receptacles placed in the same case, namely the holy chrism, a mixture of olive oil and balsam; the oil for catechumens and the oil for the sick, which are made of pure olive oil.

The only shape used today is a casket or box: therein are kept the three containers which should have the initials of the oils on their surface so that they are not mistaken one for another. The same is done on the stocks, little silver (or tin or pewter) cylindrical phials, furnished with a threaded lid, which in turn is surmounted by a cross. S.C. means holy chrism; O.I. oil for the sick (*oleum infirmorum*); O.S. or O.C. oil of the catechumens (*oleum sanctum* or *oleum catechumenorum*). A little absorbent cotton wool is placed in each of these stocks so that the oil may not spill: the priest touches the soaked cotton with his finger to take the small amount necessary for each anointing. All these vessels containing the holy oils must be carefully kept in the church or in the sacristy, in a clean and suitable place and under lock and key to prevent any profanation. There is usually a small cupboard reserved for this purpose. The oils are blessed by the bishop in his cathedral on Maundy Thursday, during the Mass of the Chrism, revived for this purpose in 1956. After this magnificent ceremony during which the pontiff is surrounded by seven subdeacons, seven deacons and twelve vested priests, the parish priests come to fill their containers for their parishes in the sacristy. Any priest may be delegated for this function but not the laity, except in the case of absolute necessity.

The qualities of the oil are to cure, enlighten, pacify and strengthen. The symbolism of this substance is specially rich and fully justifies its use for the administration of sacraments and sacramentals.

The oil for the sick, used for extreme unction, also serves to anoint bells, which, in the villages, toll to announce the last agony of Christians.

The oil of catechumens is one of the ingredients of baptismal water and is used at the administration of baptism and for the ordination of priests, for the crowning of kings and queens, for the consecration of altars. Lastly, the Holy Chrism is used for the final unction of the newly baptized, for confirmation, the consecration of bishops and for the consecration of things which are used directly for worship, such as churches, altars, chalices and patens, bells, etc.

THE ALTAR CRUETS

The wine and water which the Mass server brings to the altar are held in little receptacles, known as cruets and which are named *ampullae* or *urceoli* in liturgical books.

The two cruets for wine and water as used today date back to the thirteenth century but they are obviously a smaller version of ancient vessels, *amae*, *amulae*, such as the faithful themselves carried to the altar to offer the wine for sacrifice. Some of it was poured into the chalice, or chalices, destined for the communion of those present and the remainder was put into large vessels. When the faithful no longer communicated in the species of wine and the custom of offerings was abolished, little jars were made, often supplied with a lid, a handle and a curved tube to facilitate the pouring of the liquids. These cruets, made of gold, silver or brass, since they were similar had the great disadvantage of causing the wine and water to be confused, so the letter A (*aqua*) and V (*vinum*) were engraved on their body or lid.

Nowadays, they should be made of crystal or glass; metal ones are barely tolerated and the bishop may forbid their use in his diocese. If they are employed, they should at least be clearly distinguished, by putting a red ribbon or other indication on the wine cruet. They should be provided with a tray to match them both for the purpose of bringing them to the altar and placing them on the credence. Though in former days they were placed in a hollow cut in the side of the altar itself or inside a well cut in the wall, they must now be placed on the credence only. The Congregation of Rites does not forbid the use of a little spoon for putting water into the chalice.

THE EWER

The priest who celebrates low Mass uses the water cruet and a small basin for washing his hands; but, in certain circumstances, he may also employ the larger vessel which is customary for bishops. This is the ewer and its basin (*bacile* or *buccale*, sometimes *pelvis* and *urceus argenteus*), utensils made of engraved metal and variously adorned; they are rarely made of crystal or hard stone.

Our museums have preserved a large number of them. Jewellers outshone each other in imagination and genius when making them. They were known as *aquamaniles* and many of these vessels, which were fashionable in the fourteenth and fifteenth centuries, are sometimes shaped like knights but more often like birds or animals, such as lions, griffins or dragons.

The trays or basins were originally circular and were used both to hold the vessels and to take the water for the ablutions. Bishops wash their hands four times at pontifical Masses; before putting on the vestments, before and after the offertory and when they have finished the ablution of the chalice. They are also offered the ewer on many other occasions, especially if they have anointed with the holy oils (confirmation, ordinations of priests, consecration of churches and altars, blessings of bells, etc.) or if they have distributed blessed objects such as palms or candles. Thus, far from having a merely symbolical meaning we may say that the washing of hands has a highly practical and essential purpose.

THE PAX OR PAX BREDE

The origin of this liturgical object (called in Latin *instrumentum pacis*) is to be found in the kiss of peace which clergy and the faithful exchanged during the course of Mass.

The kiss, a sign of friendship and fraternal charity, already existed amongst the Jews and it was a very usual practice in the ordinary life of the first Christians. The apostles recommended it. St Paul concluded almost all his epistles with the words "Greet all the brethren with a holy kiss". This "holy kiss" became a solemn and religious rite, namely, the liturgical kiss which the members of the clergy still exchange at high Mass.

Up to the thirteenth century it was given as an accolade, that is to say, according to the Missal, that "the left cheeks should be placed together". But as customs became less simple men occupied one side of the nave and women the other. There were real disadvantages connected with the retention of the kiss of peace for the faithful and it was replaced by giving either a liturgical object or a holy picture to each for kissing.

Thus a cross, reliquary, Gospel book or paten were presented. In the west it was a holy image which took the form of an oval or square metal plaque on which was engraved, sculptured or enamelled, a scene of our Lord's, or the Blessed Virgin's, life or that of a saint. The relics of a saint were sometimes inserted into it in order to incite the faithful to greater devotion. Gold, silver, brass, ivory and even wood, also stone and marble, were used. Each period has naturally left its mark on these little tablets which could be so easily decorated. In the fifteenth century they often copied the shape of a portal, with pinnacled buttresses; in the time of the Renaissance they took the form of little retables with pilasters, heads of winged angels or chimeras, little statues and fanciful pediments.

Today the pax bredes, which are nearly always made of silver or gilt copper, represent the crucifixion, the entombment or resurrection of Christ. As no definite decision has been come to about this question, craftsmen have an entirely free field.

When is the pax used in liturgical ceremonies? It is presented to high dignitaries to be kissed: to a cardinal or the diocesan bishop who is present at a low Mass; to princes and magistrates at high Mass. It may also be used for the laity in such places, still quite numerous, where the custom of offering it, in any form whatever, has been preserved. It is more usually the celebrant himself who goes to the rails and offers it. This custom is sanctioned by the Congregation of Rites. It would be wrong to abandon it, wherever it exists, since it so clearly expresses the spiritual union of priests and people and the brotherly love which should reign between members of the same family.

CHAPTER IX

CHURCH BELLS

It is an interesting experience to be present at the founding of a bell. The Church is concerned in this process since the ritual contains a form of blessing which the priest pronounces while the brass is being melted and when the casting is finished. Nowadays a brick furnace is scarcely ever used. For the founding of metal hollow cubes are used, furnished with a double pivot which allows the whole furnace to incline gently at the time the cast is made.

About eighty per cent of copper is first placed in this crucible. When this is melted down tin is added, and sometimes a little antimony, zinc or lead. It was once thought that the addition of silver was conducive to improving the tone; this appears to have been simply a prejudice. It is true that, in the Middle Ages, people who were present at the process carried out near their churches were invited to throw silver pieces into the furnace. However, as Viollet-le-Duc stated, "we are easily inclined to believe that more silver went into the purses of these industrialists (the bell-founders) than into their crucibles". It is even said that this metal has never been purposely put into the bells not even into those which have a "silvery" tone.

The most troublesome operation is the making of the mould into which the molten metal is poured. The core which corresponds to the interior of the bell is first built in a square casting-pit: it is made of brick mixed with earth covered over with cement and is hollow so that coal may be burned in it. Indeed, this masonry must be carefully dried for twelve to twenty-four hours.

The second process consists in giving this core the exact shape of the bell (inner surface): a plank suitable for smoothing it is then placed in the centre and turned on a pivot. This big revolving compass or lathe is called the "strickle-board". Three or four coats of finer clay are applied to this core, the final one is a mixture of ashes and soap.

The third process: a *false bell* is then constructed using a mixture of fine sieved clay mixed with cow-hair and hemp to prevent crevices, that is to say, a very thick layer is made of the exact dimensions of the future bell. The strickle-board, which is now fitted with a curve which copies the exterior of the bell, is again set turning. A coating of tallow, soap and wax is applied before placing on it the waxen strips bearing inscriptions. For this purpose letters, numerals, figures and even coats of arms are traced in relief and, so to speak, stuck in strips on the false bell. When heat is applied the wax will obviously melt and leave hollows.

Fourth process: the mould must now be covered with a very strong covering also made of clay, which fills up the remaining space in the casting-pit.

The last process consists in withdrawing this coating, in breaking the false bell or removing it, then in replacing the coating which is completely buried. It is capped with a little mould shaped like the ears of the bell. Between the core and the covering there is now an empty space which is of the exact shape and thickness of the future bell. The molten metal having been melted for from nine to ten hours it only remains to pour it into the mould; it flows like a fiery torrent in a channel which brings it up to the top of the covering. The pouring only lasts for a few minutes but it takes a day or two to cool down.

This is a very delicate task but something more is

needed. It is rather exceptional for the bell to emit an altogether satisfactory sound when it first comes out of the casting-pit. As a matter of fact the sound of bells belongs to that category of musical sounds which are termed complex. When the clapper strikes the edge of the bronze instrument it sets in motion a great number of vibratory systems to which there are different and well-defined corresponding notes, though it is difficult to distinguish between them. A practised ear can detect up to five, and sixteen and even eighteen of them can be recorded with the help of certain instruments. How may a harmonic relation be established between these sounds, which of their nature are unrelated?

A piano string vibrates and gives a strike note corresponding to the string's total vibration. Various harmonics are superimposed, corresponding to the geometric divisions of the string. A bell, on the contrary, has no harmonics; but there are concomitant sounds in it, which, according to the bell's profile, may vary independently of each other. This is what the brothers Paccard, master-campanologists, state and they add that this profile should be studied in order to give the bronze five principal tones in the following harmonic relations: the fundamental or strike note; the "hum", thus called because of the buzzing it makes and which is an octave lower than the fundamental; the tierce above the fundamental; the fifth; finally the higher octave.

The only perfect bell, therefore, is that in which the three octaves are in strict consonance. The elements of power, sonority and richness of tone must be considered in addition to the essentially musical aspects of correctness and purity.

Luckily the founders of bells need fear no competition in the kingdom of sound. They do not confine themselves to using alloys of a well-tempered richness but they strive to balance the sounds and to regulate, as it were, their acoustic intensity. We shall not attempt to probe their manufacturing secrets which they have discovered after many long experiments. We shall be satisfied with knowing that the necessary adjustments are made by very clever workers and presuppose a special study of the material. The bell is very often shaped at the turning-lathe or its rim is ground down, thus reducing its weight.

All our modern bells have the same shape and are splayed at the bottom. This is nearly always badly represented by artists. It might be imagined that they had never seen any. But there was much groping before this shape was definitely worked out. The famous bell of Fontenailles (1202), which is preserved in the Bayeux Museum, is often quoted as the model of the modern bell. There were previously bells of very assorted shapes, very often in sheet-iron riveted together.

The origin of bells is shrouded in mystery. We need not refer to all the percussion instruments used in the days of antiquity: Egyptians, Chinese, Phoenicians, Slavs, Greeks and Romans used them for many purposes. The striking of any sort of metal will not produce the sound of a bell: it is a question of sonorous instruments only "whose sound is made by means of a clapper placed in their centre" (G. Lanoë-Villène).

What concerns us here is their liturgical use. It would really appear that monks were the first to use the *signum* (the first name for the bell) for rising and for regulating the many exercises of their life of prayer. Serious authors, such as Cardinal Bona and Abbé Pascal (1863), think that it was on the morrow of the Church's liberation, after Constantine's edict (313), that she had recourse to bells to summon the faithful to her ceremonies. A fairly widely accepted opinion formerly attributed the invention, or rather the introduction of bells into churches, to St Paulinus, bishop of Nola, near Naples in Campania (353–431). This is far from certain, because the first to use *nola*, in the sense of bell, is a person named Flodoard, who lived in the tenth century (894–966). It is possible that the term has no connection with the town of Nola.

The brass employed at that time came from Campania whose bronze industry used for many domestic utensils won well-earned fame. Thus the name *campanae, campana* in Latin and *campano* in dialect, was given to bells and remained down to our own day. The word *clocca* only appears in the seventh century, as a word from low Latin.

It is certain that reference is made to bells in 595 in the writings of St Gregory of Tours and that some authors think it was Pope Sabinian (604–6), the immediate successor of St Gregory the Great, who first prescribed their use to announce the offices. They began to sound the hours towards 605. Despite this, people had not yet become used to their sound, as is proved by the following fact.

Clotaire was besieging the town of Sens. The situation was critical. The besieged were growing weak through lack of food and Clotaire was preparing for the final assault. He had to be either repulsed at any price or panic had to be spread amongst his troops. The bishop of Orléans, who happened to be in the beleaguered town, had a sudden inspiration: he had the bells of the church of Saint-Etienne rung furiously—Clotaire's army was instantly seized with fear and "courageously" took to flight and scattered in confusion across the countryside.

During Charlemagne's reign the use of bells spread throughout Europe. All ecclesiastical writers of the ninth century speak of their ceremonial blessing. Alcuin, the great savant, whom Charlemagne endowed with three abbeys, and who founded schools at Paris, Tours and Aix-la-Chapelle, was certainly not a stranger to them. The sacred nature of Christian bells combined with the skill and ever increasing daring of the founders, rapidly increased their number. The poorest village succeeded in having its own. The Middle Ages saw the rise of "chiming towns" like Avignon, Troyes, Lisieux and Cologne.

The pealings were regulated in a very exact and very complicated manner. Edmond Martinot in his book *Les cloches des églises de Troyes* enumerates the ringing of the bells of the cathedral in 1686. The regulation in force distinguishes "annual feasts, solemn feasts, feasts of the second, third, fourth class, semi-doubles, ordinary Masses, funerals, anniversaries, etc.". On the eve of annual feasts they are rung firstly for an hour, from two to three o'clock in the afternoon; namely: two big bells for half an hour, then four small bells for a quarter of an hour, then during the last quarter of an hour the two small middles for the first peal, the chapter bell and the big middle for the second, the big middle and the bishop's bell for the third, the two big middles for the fourth, the two big ones for the fifth, and for the last a carillon of the whole six bells. For Compline the two big bells are rung from the beginning of the first psalm to the end of the last one. For the close of the day nine consecutive peals are sounded on the two big bells and "then a carillon". If this is the way the day before what will it be on the morrow? It would be tiresome to give a detailed account of all the day's ringings. The ringers were not idle in the good town of Troyes and the old Champenois adage was right: "What are they doing in Troyes? They are ringing." And there was all the more ringing since there were then something over a hundred bells in the belfries.

The monasteries, so numerous in Europe, vied with the cathedral, collegiate and parish churches. Durandus, bishop of Mende, explains that there are six kinds of bells: the *squilla* which is used in the refectory, the *nola* in the church choir, the *nonula* or double bell for the clock, the *campana* in the campanile and lastly the *signum* in the belfry tower. This enables us to find in a single sentence practically all the names given to bells. And yet we must add the little bells (*tintinnabulum*) to the list: they were the only type known to the ancients and we still use them in our sanctuaries.

The popes, adopting the practice of the Roman emperors' ancient bells, *tintinnabula imperialia*, had the Blessed Sacrament carried before them on their journeys on a white mule, with a silver-gilt bell round its neck. The bell rang as the animal moved along. This was one of the *tintinnabula papala*.

It is said that Cardinal Guido, papal legate to Germany, first originated the ringing of the bell at the moment of the consecration. Today it is obligatory for the server at the *Sanctus*, at the two elevations and, in many places, before the priest's communion. We need not mention the optional ringings which have been added to those prescribed. There is usually to be found a *tintinnabulum* or in any case a little bell, hanging on the sacristy door: it should be rung at the beginning of each Mass and office, when the celebrant leaves to go to the altar.

The sacristan or server sounds a small bell when he accompanies the priest who is carrying the Holy Viaticum to the sick. Doubtless this immemorial custom has fallen into disuse in many places, yet it is still in force in many Christian countries where the sense of sacred things still lives on.

BELFRIES

The bells were not originally placed in the churches themselves but on towers apart from them. They were rung by striking them with a hammer or mallet. Then they were attached to the keystone of a window or hung from the church rafters. The clapper gradually came into general use, the bells became mobile and were set moving firstly by a rope which was pulled and later by a pedal.

Belfries made their appearance in the eleventh and twelfth centuries. They replaced the old ringers' towers where the "bellman" kept watch.

They were housed in appropriate quarters in a sort of look-out turret surmounting the roof. The custom of building "campaniles" outside churches developed in Italy; lastly, joined to the main building the belfries became part of the body of the Gothic cathedral, the soul of which was the bell. Nowadays, certain belfries overlook their church from a great height; but it is preferable that they should stand a little higher than the highest part of the nave. The neighbouring buildings and grounds will have the same acoustic effect on their resonance as has a hall on a piano or violin.

It is advisable to build thick walls and to arrange openings towards the top to facilitate the path of the sound waves. If luffer boards which have too pronounced a slope are put on the bays they send the sound brusquely earthwards and the result is a discordant noise instead of a musical harmony. The bells, when mounted on a solid scaffolding independent of the walls, can sound a peal, a big peal and a full peal, that is to say that the clapper, which has a different centre of gravity, strikes the two edges successively. The whole metal trembles and gives an impression of coming to life, according to the variation of intensity and tonality which these rapid strokes set up in the inside of the sonorous chamber.

What about the carillons, whose name comes from the low Latin *quadrilio* (quaternary) because the original ones had only four bells? Today they have up to five or six octaves. Master change-ringers, who are real artists, can play quite a variety of airs upon them. The carillon is Flanders' national musical instrument: the most famous are those of Bruges, Malines, Ghent and Antwerp. In Holland the most renowned are those of Amsterdam, Delft and Harlem. Their number has lately increased in France, and in other parts of the world.

The change-ringers' task has fortunately been lightened by the widespread use of electricity. They can now use keyboards like those of organs. They are a great advance on pedals which had to be struck with a mallet or the fist. The bells are also set in motion electrically in many churches. An automatic system enables them to ring a change as desired or to toll or again to sound the three Angelus peals at the customary hours. Since Pius XII had the bells of St Peter's in Rome electrified there can be no further argument about the lawfulness or suitability of this modern method. Yet mechanism must not be allowed to suppress the living element in our chimings. It must be admitted that the tone of the bells is no longer what it was, mechanical regularity militates against the "flexible and expressive nature given to the bell by a human agency". M. Bayart suggests that we should at least keep one real ringer dressed in a surplice, for the elevation, for instance. In any case we must choose a system which includes the possibility of pulling a rope.

Indeed there is a serious disadvantage in being dependent on a meter and a generating station. Should the electric current happen to fail momentarily, then the light suddenly goes out, the bells stop and the organ dies out.

There are no liturgical rules concerning the number of bells to be set in motion nor the way they should be rung. There is reference only to the *festive note* and the *mourning note*. It could never be allowed that the tolling for the dead should be the same as for feasts, the arrival and departure of the bishop or when a procession leaves or enters the church.

The local custom should be followed everywhere. In many places a slow pealing announces a person's agony or death; the knell is sounded, that is to say, a single bell at regular intervals or the successive pealing of several between the death and burial, according to established custom. For instance, two strokes for women, three for men, one for children and, for clergy, as many strokes as they have received orders. This funereal tolling is forbidden by the Congregation of Rites during all feasts when funeral Masses are prohibited, from the evening of the vigil and the

whole of the following day. Everybody knows that all bells
are mute in every church and chapel of the Catholic world
from Maundy Thursday until Easter Eve.

THE BLESSING OF BELLS

The Church, who sanctifies all she touches, could hardly
fail to bless the bells which are so intimately associated
with her worship. From the beginning and down to our
own days this liturgical function has been reserved to the
bishop: a priest cannot do so except as the bishop's delegate. We must distinguish between *the blessing of the
metal*, of which we spoke in connection with the manufacturing process, and the *blessing of bells designed for
profane use*, such as town-belfry, school establishments, etc.
A third formula may be found in our Roman Ritual for
bells of *churches and chapels which have been merely
blessed and not consecrated*. The most solemn formula
which is reserved for consecrated churches and chapels
may be found in the Pontifical.

This ceremony was referred to from very early times, as
the "baptism of the bells", but a protest was raised against
such an improper and metaphorical expression. A capitu-
lary of Charlemagne forbids the "baptism" of bells (not
their blessing), because certain practices tended to merge
these rites with the sacrament of baptism. Now, it is
superfluous to point out that this is not a sacrament but a
simple blessing, a kind of dedication such as is performed
for our churches. Its purpose is to withdraw these objects
from all profane use, to consecrate them to God and his
service, and to make them, in as far as he so wills, the
instruments of his graces and favours. But it cannot at the
same time be denied that the liturgical function resembles
the sacrament of Christian initiation in many respects: the
bell is sprinkled, and even washed, in holy water and is
anointed with holy oil. "As to god-parents for the names
given to bells these are medieval inventions over which

we need not linger," we read in Dom Leclercq's *Diction-
naire d'archéologie chrétienne et de liturgie.*

The blessing of bells, exclusive of those used in clocks,
is strictly obligatory, and it should be done before the bells
are hoisted up to the campanile or belfry. From that day
onwards it is forbidden to put them to profane use. The
only exception to this is in case of public calamities when
it is a matter of calling for immediate help, as in the case
of fires, floods or other impending dangers.

Doubtless bells no longer mark the tempo of the civil
life of cities and villages as they formerly did. They no
longer announce municipal meetings, the opening and
ending of fairs, the punishment of criminals; they have
ceased to peal forth in order to avert hailstones and frost.
Small and large cattle-bells are no longer hung from the
beasts' necks in the majority of countrysides. They have
fallen silent like the harness-bells of horse vehicles. But
bells still fulfil their liturgical mission, they ring out rarely
and hoarsely when persecution rages but frequently and
joyously where liberty reigns. They sing the baptism of the
newly-born; through the Angelus they regulate the worker's
labour, they hail the founding of a new household, they
call the faithful together on Sundays. They announce the
last agony of the sick in muffled knells; they remind the
faithful to join in prayer with the death throes of the dying;
they bid the dead a last farewell on behalf of the Christian
community. Thus the sonorous bronze mingles with our
family life, shares in our religious life and is associated
with our national life; it has become the carillon of victory
and it reinforces the hymn of the *Te Deum* with its vibrat-
ing tones. Henry Reverdy writes:

> If ever, which God forbid, the bells fell silent, a whole
> section of our family and social life would be muted. It
> would be as if we were deprived of the means of expressing
> our emotions collectively. Neither song, instrumental music,
> nor even the organ have the same simplicity nor the same

breadth of appeal. The chiming of bells, like the very wind itself, hovers and soars over countrysides, cities and dwellings: it penetrates everywhere and reaches the very innermost depths of souls. That is why poets have sung the bells' praises and every heart responds to their poetry. Exiles cherish them as an echo of their birth place and when a traveller comes home again the chiming of his church bell, his baptism bell, arouses his tenderest emotions.

PART II

VESTMENTS

CHAPTER X

CLERICAL COSTUME

The history of costume, the traditions of each country and the fashions of each age, prove conclusively that clothing is not solely a matter of decency, convenience, well-being and hygiene. It seems to be determined far more by the desire to adopt an exterior behaviour in harmony with the ambitions or qualities of the soul. We strive, by our dress, to become what we are not by nature. The Latin word *habitus* may be as aptly applied to the moral dispositions which embellish the soul as to the outward bearing and the costume which clothes the body.

The Christian intends to imitate Christ, his divine model. He, therefore, attempts to shape his soul's behaviour according to the qualities which he sees in the transcendent personage described for us in the Gospels. This being so, should he not also follow Christ in the matter of clothing the body? There is obviously no question of copying the costume which Jesus wore during his mortal life, but rather of assuming at the time of Christian initiation a symbolical dress expressive of the invisible change by which his soul has derived such benefit. Was it not to this ritual sign that St Paul alluded when he wrote: "All you who have been baptized in Christ's name have put on the person of Christ" (Gal. 3. 27)?

The first Christians made no mistake about this: they dressed neophytes in long snow-white robes as a token of this regeneration of the whole being, this transformation of interior life which baptism brings about. Although this robe is often replaced by an ordinary white veil, the Church, even in our times, makes the new Christian put on a special attire when he comes out of the baptismal font, by telling him through the priest: "Receive this white robe which you will present without stain before the tribunal of our Lord Jesus Christ, so that you may obtain eternal life." Was not this, in truth, the first liturgical dress worn at the dawn of Christianity and which we still put on at the beginning of our Christian life?

This dazzling whiteness signifies purity of heart, virginal candour, incorruptibility of doctrine, strength of perfection. It is the image of faith and of sincerity. Thus attired, the neophytes of the primitive Church received from the bishop the laying on of hands and the anointing with holy oil in the chapel of anointment. Then, a lighted candle in their hands, a reflection of the uncreated light in the mirror of their souls, they advanced slowly, with glowing hearts, along the walls of the great basilica in order to make their first communion. It is still the custom for little girls who approach the holy table for the first time to wear white. Nowadays a white dress still adorns the radiant young woman who comes to church to receive the sacrament of marriage and it is also used by the Christian virgin who enters into a mystical union with the divine Bridegroom. This wedding garment, referred to in the Gospel in the parable of the marriage feast, therefore, is still worn by young brides as also by consecrated virgins. Why should we not call it, in the broadest sense of the word, a liturgical vestment?

THE CASSOCK

We do not imagine that the apostles and their successors wore special clothes for living and for the celebration of worship. They, like their master, dressed in the talaric robe (reaching to the ankles) which was customary in Palestine. It is even admitted that during the first five centuries of

our era the clergy's attire did not differ from that of the
ordinary faithful. St Augustine was dressed like everyone
else. St Ambrose says that it is by his charity and his
functions that we recognize a bishop and not by his clothes.
Following the barbaric invasions, the laity gradually abandoned the traditional Roman and oriental dress in favour
of the invaders' short clothes. The fashion changed, but the
members of the clergy continued to wear only the long wide
robes (*tunica talaris*) in which the faithful were accustomed
to see them.

This robe is none other than the cassock or soutane,
whose Latin name *subtanea* (nether robe) clearly shows
that it is intended for wearing underneath the sacred vestments. It is much more like a tunic than a Roman toga.

"Though the habit does not make the monk," the Council of Trent was to say, "the clergy nevertheless should
always wear clothes which suit the order they have received
and the honour and purity of their morals should be
reflected in the exterior decency of their attire."

In Latin countries the special dress of ministers of
religion arouses no surprise. Rarely even in certain localities do we find ill-mannered people asking, "Why don't they
dress like everybody else?" How can we explain to them
that priests were formerly "dressed like others" and that
they have not changed their ways? It is rather these
ignorant questioners, in short dress and with their legs
crammed into trousers, who have followed the barbarous
custom and are no longer "dressed like all the others".

The cassock is really a church garment and if the custom
of donning it for everyday wear has prevailed (in France,
Belgium, Italy, Spain, etc.), on the other hand it only
appears inside churches and other places of worship in
countries with Protestant majorities. Out of doors Catholic
priests and Protestant clergymen wear an ordinary suit,
generally black, with a special collar and no tie. This is
the clerical dress.

Doubtless in wartime, officer or soldier priests and even

military chaplains are sometimes obliged to celebrate Mass without putting on a cassock.

The cassock is therefore a clerical hallmark. It is first worn on the day when the tonsure is received, that is, when the bishop cuts a few locks from the candidate and shows him by this action that he is henceforth a member of the clergy. Tonsure and cassock are two co-related things which cannot be divorced. The cassock is not put on the candidate by the bishop and until recently was not blessed. The new Roman Ritual has a new formula for blessing the clerical dress, if it is wished to do so. At all events, though the cassock is a constitutive element of clerical dress, it does not therefore follow that it cannot be provisionally used by others, in fact the laymen who are employed in churches or who replace clerics are obliged to wear it during the performance of their functions. Such is the case for sacristans, cantors, servers and the choirmaster or choir-boys.

The colour of cassocks has varied down the centuries. It was not formerly forbidden to wear red, violet, white, green or blue cassocks. The canons of certain chapters enjoyed this privilege for a long time and there are some in Italy who still do so. In the Anglican Church it is quite usual to see different colours. It was not until the thirteenth century that the use of red and green cassocks was forbidden, first by the Council of Avignon in 1209 and then by the Council of the Lateran (1215) which, however, maintained the bishop's right to red, blue and green cassocks. St Charles Borromeo ordered his clergy to wear a near-black colour. Several provincial Councils, since then, like that of Milan, designated black for priests and lower clerics. This only affected secular clergy, for monks have kept the traditional colours of the Middle Ages, at least as regards white (Cistercians, Dominicans, Premonstratensians, etc.) and brown (Carmelites, Franciscans, Capuchins, etc.). We shall see that current legislation reserves violet for bishops and red for cardinals.

CHAPTER XI

CHOIR DRESS

The members of the clergy who, though not officiating, are present at religious ceremonies take their place in the choir stalls in the seats allotted to them. They wear a special vestment in keeping with their rank in the ecclesiastical hierarchy. This "choir dress" is in white linen, cambric, muslin or lawn. Its cut varies according to countries but it may be said that it derives from the ancient tunic. This is the linen *alb* (thus named because of its white colour; *alba*, white) which was more or less shortened and which turned into the surplice, the cotta and the rochet.

In cold climates the wide-sleeved surplice was adopted. At the time when church heating was unheard of the clergy wore a furry robe which was called *pelliceum* (pelisse). The choir dress was usually large enough to cover the fur, whence the name *super pelliceum* (superpelisse) corrupted to surplice.

Elsewhere it was the cotta which prevailed. It is still shorter and it stops at the waist while the sleeves only reach to the elbows.

The bishop himself hands the surplice to the young men during the ceremony of the first tonsure of which we spoke in connection with the cassock. He first addresses God and asks him to bless "these new servants, on whom we are about to bestow the religious habit, in your name. Grant that, by your grace, they may persevere in their devotion to the Church's service and may thus merit life without end". In investing each ordinand with this holy livery the pontiff says, "May the Lord clothe you in the new man who has been created in God's image in justice and true holiness". Those who have just been admitted to the clerical state already resemble priests exteriorly. If they have a right to ecclesiastical privileges from now onwards they also bind themselves to lead a holy and virtuous life which will redound to and increase the honour of the priesthood. Their transformation must not consist of merely exterior show but their heart "freed from earthly shackles and worldly desires" should become ever more inclined towards supernatural riches.

Clerical dignitaries wear a special choir dress, the rochet. Whatever its origin it is similar to an alb cut short at the knees. It is usually ornamented with lace. It was formerly confined to bishops, but many prelates now use it and it even forms part of the choir dress worn by canons, by a special concession of the Holy See. The latter, however, may not make use of it outside their diocese. The rochet is never put on by itself: a part of it may be seen when the bishop wears a mozzetta but it disappears almost completely under the mantelletta which the latter uses outside his diocese and which is the choir dress of most prelates. The decoration of the rochet consists of fairly wide lace borders at the end and at the wrists, sometimes at the shoulders. A material of the same colour as the cassock, violet or red, is usually placed under the lace-work at the wrists. Monks have their own special choir dress. More often than not it is a type of very full toga, the cowl. It is a woollen garment provided with wide sleeves and only opens at the top to pull on over the head. Its colour varies according to Orders: white for Cistercians, Camaldolese, Olivetans and Premonstratensians, black for the Benedictines and the Basilians, blue for the Sylvestrines, etc.

As we remarked concerning the cassock, cantors, church employees and lay servers may and even ought to wear choir dress when carrying out their duties. This is the surplice or the cotta, according to local custom. The cantors can no longer be seen in many churches because they have been moved up to a gallery near the west door. Needless to say the question of choir dress does not arise in their case but this situation is very much to be deplored and bishops have often regretted it. The normal place for the choir (or schola) is near the sanctuary and not aloft and far from the congregation of the faithful. Its members really form part of the community at prayer and inspire it by their singing. They play a very important liturgical rôle since they must lead the choral performance of those assisting at Mass and interpret the most difficult pieces in their midst. They were formerly grouped around the lectern, which was placed in the centre of the choir, and they occupied the lower stalls, nearest this assembly point, as monks still do.

Lastly, we cannot overlook a custom which has become very widespread during the last forty years. The reappearance of young choristers or school choir pupils throughout the world is of immense benefit for Catholic worship; some have adopted the alb as a choir dress. The effect of this garment which reaches to the heels, like the Roman tunics, and is caught in at the waist by a sash is very striking, and owing to its simplicity is in perfect harmony with the surplices and cottas of the clergy.

THE ALMUCE, THE MOZETTA, THE CAPE

Choir dress is usually completed by a woollen garment which covers the upper part of the body, the shoulders and the head and is known by the name of almuce, mozzetta or cape. These three forms certainly derive from the choir cope or *cappa*, a large mantle worn by most canons in winter-time. In olden days as there was little or no heating of churches and as both the day and night offices were very long, it was not possible to remain in the stalls without being warmly clad in wool. The cappa which was often fur-lined was prescribed for all clerics or canons—this last name was applicable to all the clergy. The children of the *schola cantorum* were counted amongst the latter. This indoor mantle gradually became the badge of cathedral or collegiate chapters while the name of canon itself became an honorary title. In the Dominican order, formerly one of regular canons, the novice was always invested with the cappa when being clothed in his habit, and the prior, who conferred these religious insignia upon him, also wore it for this function.

The hood was gradually brought out to the front revealing precious fur in winter and silken lining in summer. The mantle developed a train in modern times and a cleric was assigned to carry it. It will be referred to in the chapter on episcopal vesture. The canons of a large number of chapters were honoured by permission to wear this prelate's cappa. Since they were not entitled to employ clerics for carrying the train, they lifted it up, folded it and twisted it round their arm. The cappa, thus distorted, was so very dissimilar from its primitive form that a pious canon, who wished to find a mystical meaning for the choir dress, asserts, in a treatise on asceticism, that the canonical cappa which had to be wound round the arm represents the bonds with which our Lord was loaded during his passion. Much the same has happened to the almuce, a furred winter cape lined with more fur. Its logical use would seem to be to protect one's shoulders and head. Unfortunately where it is still in use it is merely worn on the left arm as a cumbersome badge. In the Premonstratensian Order, the deacon up to this very day lays it down on the altar during high Mass. The ancient furred hood has been called an almuce though it is now no more than a little pocket about eight inches square.

The almuce in fabric which was usually smaller gave rise to the mozzetta, which effectively covers the trunk of the body and is fastened down the breast with a line of buttons. In Rome it is called almucetta, mosetta, that is, small mozzetta or almutia for cardinals. In France the word *camail* (cape) has been retained, especially for priests and seminarists who wear it in choir. From being a plain hood, this head-gear soon came down to the shoulders, increased in size and was furnished with strips of fur or velour, in imitation of the almuce.

The hood, on the other hand, replaced by the biretta, became so small that it could not be used. Shrivelled up and atrophied it looks exactly like "a little wooden bowl clinging to the back" (Dom H. Leclercq).

It is wiser not to speak of the colour of this cape because dioceses have adopted so many different shades: red, violet, purple, black, the linings often being of a contrasting colour. The black camail is also adorned with various edgings, as an indication of the rank held in the ecclesiastical hierarchy.

THE BIRETTA, THE SKULL CAP

The layman's head covering has varied according to the whims of fashion. On the other hand the different societies of men of learned professions, such as judges and doctors, have retained the shape of that formerly worn by them. The round supple woollen cap which came into fashion in the fourteenth century is evidently derived from them. Its wear was made compulsory by the ecclesiastical authorities, though the use of the almuce was optional. Towards the end of the following century the former was definitely ousted by the square cap. The word *biretum* (perhaps a diminutive of *birrus*, hood) came from the dents formed by the fingers of the right hand when putting it on and taking it off: *bisrectum*, which gave *beretta* in Italian and *béret* in French. This accounts for the three protrusions which sometimes cause astonishment and which really originated with the two depressions in the material.

With the exception of Spain, where it remains pliable, the biretta has been lined with buckram or cardboard. This has established the square shape and has emphasized the three ridges in the form of an arc.

The doctors' biretta still exists, but is rarely used. It has four ridges in order to distinguish it from the clerical biretta. It is used by both clerics and laity; it may not be used in church ceremonies but only for academic meetings and teaching.

The clerical biretta is always made of black cloth or merino for all priests and clerics. We shall see that bishops and cardinals wear violet or red ones. Canons, according to the particular constitution of their chapters, often decorate their birettas with coloured edgings, borders and tassels. It is part of the choir dress but it is also used with the sacred vestments. In the first case it is not worn when walking but when seated or in processions outside the church. On the other hand those who are vested wear it when walking, for instance, every time they are going to or coming from a liturgical function.

In the *Ceremonial of Bishops* biretta is used indifferently for biretta and skull cap. The latter, in fact, derives from the former: it is much smaller nowadays. As often happens it originally served a practical purpose: the clergy used it to cover their ecclesiastical tonsure, that is, the crown-like shaven surface of the whole top of the head. It became a mark of honour, status or dignity. Priests may still wear it on all occasions but they must have special permission from the Holy See to celebrate Mass in it. And, like prelates who use it, they must take it off during certain parts of the holy sacrifice, particularly from the consecration to the people's communion. It is made of black cloth for all ecclesiastics who are not bishops.

CHAPTER XII

THE VESTMENTS OF ORDAINED MINISTERS

LINEN VESTMENTS COMMON TO ALL OFFICIANTS

Though priests at the beginning of Christianity used the same clothes as other citizens for everyday wear, that does not mean that "sacred vestments" as distinct from "usual clothes" did not already exist. We need only refer, amongst other proofs, to the fact that Stephen I († 257) forbade the use of liturgical dress for workaday purposes. This can be read in the former ninth lesson of August 2nd in the Roman breviary. Moreover, it was a reminder of an ancient custom, violated by some clerics, that the pope wished particularly to enjoin. The type and cut of these sacred vestments must have been like those of ordinary clothes but they were probably distinguished from them by the richness of the material and the care taken to reserve them for sacred functions.

We know for certain that this costume was made up of two garments: the *linea* which was white, and the *byrrhus*, of a dark colour, brown, purple or black. The first had sleeves and the second was sleeveless. The undergarment was of woven linen with falling folds moulded to the shape of the body on which it was placed, while the outer garment made of cloth which could be of the richest quality, was designed as a real garment, a mantle or dress.

Jerome Carcopino asserts that "the ancients distinguished between two kinds of garments, those which are put on and those which are wrapped around the body afterwards". The *indumenta* are worn day and night, while the *amictus* is only put on for part of the day. All our liturgical vesture is modelled on that of polite Roman society of the last days of the Empire, that is, of the fourth and fifth centuries.

The *jocale* which was worn round the neck and on the shoulders, as a protection against the cold or sweat, has become our amice. It is really a rectangular linen cloth provided with two braids or ribbons which allow it to be fastened round the body. It is used by all who wear the alb and is put on first underneath it. When doing duty as assistant deacons at Mass or at pontifical Vespers canons put it on over their rochet and priests over their surplice.

The ancient *linea*, which became the *indumentum* par excellence, was a sort of roomy shirt made of two flaps sewn together. It was used by both men and women up to the sixth century and it is from this that our alb derived. Although it was abandoned by the laity clerics continued to use it for religious worship. Curiously enough it is perhaps the only garment which has not changed its shape, since it suffered none of the transformations and reductions which have altered the primitive simplicity of the other items of liturgical costume.

Artisans, travellers and soldiers of antiquity had the habit of fastening the *linea* around their waists and, when working or walking, of holding it up, when necessary, by a *cingulum* or belt made of leather or cloth. During a long period the clergy wore coloured belts embellished with woven or embroidered designs, or sometimes even jewellery, pearls or precious stones, golden or silver threads. In the Latin Church, this useful ornament has been replaced by the very simple cord which is used today. It should properly be of linen or hemp like the other portions of the liturgical vesture but it may also be made of wool or silk

of the same colour as the feast-day being celebrated or of
the religious season. The cord is the indispensable com-
plement of the alb. All officiants, priest, deacon and subdeacon wear these three principal garments, the amice, the
alb and the cord, over their cassock.

SILKEN VESTMENTS PROPER TO ORDAINED MINISTERS

The liturgical vestments which are specially connected
with ordained ministers are the tunicle and the dalmatic.
The first is conferred on the subdeacon, the second on the
deacon, on the day of their ordination.

These garments had their origin in the lay world and
were even reserved for senators at the end of the fourth
century. They were assigned to the higher ranks of the
hierarchy, excepting priests, and principally to the episcopate. Besides, at the beginning and even for quite a number
of centuries these two tunics were white, the noblest of all
colours, evoking the idea of joy, justice and perfection. And
this is the symbolism assigned to the pontiff's action when
he confers one or other of these garments on his ministers,
but it should be noted that they have a different origin.

The tunicle

The Romans sometimes wore two tunics, one over the
other: the first was the ordinary attire of common servants;
the second (the *colobus*) came as far as the knees and had
either no sleeves or very short ones. We imagine that the
subdeacon's tunicle derives from this garment used in
everyday life, but reserved for solemn occasions, as a
precious alb would be. This tunic was called *linea
dalmatica* and *dalmatica minor* and was a sort of a midway
garment between the alb and the dalmatic. In the tenth
century, at all events, it was clearly distinguished from the
two other garments.

Nowadays it is still too often cut on the same pattern as

the dalmatic. The mere fact that it is suited to an inferior rank should lead vestment makers to distinguish it. Are they aware that the tunicle should be shorter than the dalmatic, that its sleeves, on the contrary, should be longer and, above all, that it should be only very plainly decorated? We need merely refer to the *Ceremonial of Bishops*, which describes it. The subdeacon should wear a tunicle when fulfilling his functions except on the Sundays of Advent and Lent and on several other well-defined occasions. If there is no subdeacon available, a cleric of a lower rank, dressed in the same way, may sing the epistle and perform several rites of the former's office. It is absolutely forbidden to extend this latitude to the laity.

The dalmatic

The dalmatic, a garment with sleeves like the preceding one, betrays its origin by its very name. It came from Dalmatia, a Greek province, during the republican era. In Rome it partially ousted the famous toga, which was not very comfortable to wear. It is said that the Emperors Diocletian, Heliogabalus and Commodus were fond of starting exotic fashions publicly and at the circus. The dalmatic, having being adopted by the patriarchs of Constantinople, was at first conferred, as a mark of honour, on some bishops of famous sees, then on archdeacons and finally on all deacons. Pope Silvester (314–35) is said to have conferred it on the Roman deacons and it gradually became the regular costume of the lowest ordained minister. Nevertheless, though it was a dress of distinction, it continued to be a profane garment until the seventh century, worn by emperors and consuls and, later on, by French kings.

The dalmatic is longer than the tunicle, with wider and shorter sleeves; it is an outside garment. It was unfortunately shortened and split down the side, first as far as the knees to facilitate walking, then up as far as under the arms; its sleeves were also cut lengthwise and fastened by ribbons. The ribbons disappeared and the shrunken sleeves became mere flaps. Real sleeves have never been abandoned in Italy and the sides of the garment only open near the bottom. Happily this normal pattern has been restored in many places.

As regards ornamentation, it follows tradition. Two bands of purple cloth, called *clavi*, reach from the shoulders to the bottom, in front and behind. Representations of these *clavi* are often found in the catacombs. In that which was discovered under the Latin Way in 1955 nearly all the personages painted on the walls are dressed in tunics with *clavi*. This would lead us to believe that in the first half of the fourth century—which is the date suggested by the secretary of the Pontifical Commission of sacred archaeology—all Romans, men and women, wore only this long dress (*Civiltà cattolica*, April 21st, 1956). In view of this evidence it would be wrong to seek to add other ornamentation or to do the same to the subdeacon's tunicle.

Lastly, since the dalmatic together with the tunicle always form part of the "pontificals" donned by the bishop when he sings Mass, it still remains in the nature of a privilege for the deacon: he only wears it on feast-days. Furthermore, for certain functions he confines himself to the deacon's stole, which is his own distinctive vestment and the only one used by deacons in the Carthusian Order.

CHAPTER XIII

INSIGNIA

THE MANIPLE

Insignia are outward marks, most often distinctive items of dress, which indicate the rank occupied in the hierarchy. For officiants of the Catholic liturgy there are two insignia, the *maniple* and the *stole*. The subdeacon at his ordination receives the maniple and he retains it on proceeding to the other major orders. In the same way when he becomes a deacon the bishop invests him with the stole. Raised to the dignity of the priesthood and even of the episcopacy he will still wear this distinctive vestment. Worn by bishops, priests, deacons and subdeacons at Mass, the maniple consists of a silken band which nearly always ends in a fringe. It is attached to the left fore-arm and is of no practical use; it is quite evident that it is a distinguishing mark for those who have received major orders.

What is its origin? Jerome Carcopino, the author of learned works and in particular of one on daily life in Rome, describes meals of the imperial era. All the guests reclined on couches with room for three, the left elbow resting on a cushion. Each of the guests brought his own napkin (it was not supplied by the host as is now the fashion) in order to avoid soiling the covering of the couch. Knives and spoons, but not forks, were used. It was the custom to eat with one's fingers and slaves circulated frequently with ewers or basins for washing the hands.

The *mappula* or table-napkin was therefore used to wipe them, as well as the mouth. Convention did not forbid the guests to carry away a napkin full of titbits which they had no time to eat. Otherwise, the cloth was folded up at the end of the meal and placed between the fingers or on the left arm.

This is the usual explanation. Others have been suggested: a *mappa* (a Carthaginian word which also means napkin) was worn by women hanging from the left arm. It was used to wipe dust and sweat from their faces. Possibly it was also used for the nose according to a custom whose origin should not be dated too far back, since the only Latin word which could be correctly translated by handkerchief (*muccinum*) does not appear before the end of the third century of our era.

There was also a ceremonial napkin (*mappa* or *mappula*) which in the fourth century became a luxury and also the distinctive consular mark. Several diptychs represent the consul holding it in his right hand and waving it to give the starting signal for races at the circus. Cassiodorus relates that the emperor Nero, while dining in the Golden House which overlooked the Circus Maximus, took his table-napkin and flung it through the window as a signal for the races. From that day the *mappa* became the mark of a consul. The spectators in the amphitheatre itself waved them to show their enthusiasm. The emperor Aurelius distributed supplies to the people so that they might applaud their favourite charioteers and actors.

It seems to have taken a long time for these napkins to turn into mere embroidered bands. For a considerable time the clerics (this appears to have applied to all clerics regardless of their rank) retained it for use in liturgical functions. St Clement I is depicted on the mural painting of his Roman basilica holding his *mappula* between the thumb and first finger of his left hand.

Deacons covered their left hand with it, subdeacons held

the paten between its ends, while acolytes used it to give
or receive the objects used in worship.

In the eighteenth century, the choir-boys of the church
of Saint-Jean at Lyons still carried it between the fingers of
the left hand while they were singing the Holy Saturday
prophecies. Even today in the Lyons liturgy clerics still
hold a maniple as they sing the lessons which, in certain
Masses, precede the Epistle.

Subdeacons did not receive the *mappula* on their ordination until the eleventh century. It soon came to be univer-
sally accepted as their characteristic badge, really distinctive to their order. But the word itself was distorted into
manipula, manus pleo, what is taken by the handful, that
which fills the hand. Hence the symbolism of the "sheaves
of wheat" to which the psalmist refers (Ps. 125) and consequently of the bunches of flowers or grass, of stems or
vine-shoots, which has certainly inspired the formula of
investiture for the subdiaconate: "Receive the maniple
which symbolizes the fruit of good works."

Thus, this cloth used for cleansing became a band of
more or less ornamented silk and lost its utilitarian purpose
completely: no one dared to use it any longer. The maniple
subsequently became quite large, was laden with embroideries, precious stones, golden or silver bands. Its
fringes, which are certainly its finest feature, were sometimes turned into pyriform tassels, which were a regular
treasury of embroidery and jewellery. Unfortunately its
ends were widened into the shape of trapezoidal blades,
ugly large shovels or bats, heavily decorated. But, for some
years now, a simpler form has come into use consisting of
two narrow and parallel sections with little or no
decoration.

The origin of the *mappula* and the symbolical meaning
which the maniple acquired both seem to be recalled in
the formula which the priest recites when placing it on his
arm: "Grant, O Lord that I may be worthy to wear the

maniple of tears and sorrow so that I may joyfully receive the reward of my work."

The present ceremonial has also retained the primitive meaning of a table-napkin for this badge. "The early Christians," says Rohault de Fleury, "who borrowed so much from domestic customs for their growing liturgy, probably had the idea of bringing the ordinary festal utensils to the eucharistic banquet—we may well imagine that they did the same for hand-towels."

Thus, the bishop always receives the maniple at the moment when he goes up to the altar (except at Masses for the dead). The priest who administers the sacrament of marriage and afterwards celebrates Mass, wears the stole and chasuble to receive the consent of the parties and what follows; he does not don the maniple until he begins Mass. The deacons at the throne of a solemn pontifical Mass wear no maniple, because they have no function to perform at the altar during the holy sacrifice.

Likewise, there are two occasions on which the priests wear the chasuble without stole or maniple, because they take no part in the Mass: at the Corpus Christi procession and when carrying the bier for the relics at the consecration of a church. On the other hand, the twelve priests who assist the bishop on Maundy Thursday for the blessing of the holy oils, wear the maniple together with the stole and chasuble because in primitive days they concelebrated with the bishop. Thus, though it has not retained its original function the maniple is specially reserved for the Eucharistic banquet.

THE STOLE

Bishops, priests and deacons wear round the neck a long silken band whose ends reach down approximately to the knees and sometimes lower. The stole is the distinctive mark of the power of order, worn by those who have received the episcopate, the priesthood or the diaconate. It should be noted, however, that they do not all wear it in the same way. A bishop always lets the two sides of the stole hang parallel to each other before him, while the priest, when clad in the alb, places them across his breast. On the other hand, the deacon puts the stole on his left shoulder like a scarf, so that one length comes across his breast and the other across his back, with the ends meeting under his right arm.

There is no other distinctive mark indicating the rank in the ecclesiastical hierarchy by the *mere manner of wearing it*.

Experts disagree about the origin of the stole. Some wished to consider it as a substitute for the Jewish prayer-mantle, others as the border of the ancient *stola*, worn by Roman ladies, which was a full-length dress with sleeves and opening in the front. The embroidered or gold-threaded bands would have been separated from the garment itself (*stola*, garment) to which they were attached or sewn. The question arises as to how the *stola*, which had disappeared after the sixth century, could have given its name to these bands which decorated it and which would have become detached from it. Dom Leclercq has replied authoritatively to this hypothesis: "This is an interesting fancy, but only a fancy. In order to contract a robe to such an extent as to reduce it to a thin strap monuments and texts must be disregarded, because not a single one of these has been quoted in support of such a strange transformation."

Moreover, the word *stola* did not appear until the Carolingian period. Until then all Christian writers used the word *orarium* to designate it.

We much prefer the explanation given by the majority of liturgists who regard it as a narrow scarf, called indiscriminately in Greek, *orarion* and *omophorion*. The former has been retained by the Greeks to this very day and meant a cloth worn round the neck like a muffler. It was intended for wiping the mouth (*os, oris*), drying sweat and, when necessary, tears (*sudarium*).

It may be seen, moreover, on many pagan monuments placed around the neck of certain figures and reaching to the breast like a tie or a scarf. Its use seems to have been confined to people of rank such as pontiffs, princes, priestesses, dignitaries, Roman ladies. The common people were satisfied to use the flap of their mantle for wiping their face and neck.

In the catacombs the Good Shepherd himself is pictured with a double ribbon in the form of a cross, and the *orantes* wear a similar strap on their shoulders. On a fifth-century mosaic funeral slab at Thabraca, the defunct Dardonius lies among flowers, between two candles; he has an *orarium*, embroidered with rosettes and ending in fringes, around his neck (Dom Leclercq). An orante named Cresconia is dressed in a blue dalmatic and white narrow-fringed stole; the presence of yellow *clavi* which reach down to the bottom of the dalmatic is sufficient proof of the distinction which should be made between *clavi* and the *orarium*. We may add that St Augustine, in *The City of God* (in 426), tells the strange story of a boy whose eye was wrenched from its socket and hung down his cheek by a thread; the unfortunate lad put his eye back in its place as best he could and bandaged it with his *orarium*. He therefore wore this cloth which he was able to use as an improvised dressing.

All this evidence shows that the stole was really a sort of muffler used by the laity, men, women and children. The luxurious *orarium* was a mark of special distinction. We thus see it, as from the fifth century, around bishops' and patriarchs' necks. Isidore of Pelusium (first half of the sixth century) said that the *orarium*, woven in wool, recalled the lost sheep placed on the Good Shepherd's shoulders.

Having turned into a distinguishing mark, the linen or woollen *omophorium* was replaced by a silken band and was no longer suited to its primitive purpose. It gradually acquired ornaments especially at its ends which hung down below the liturgical vestments, the priest's chasuble or the deacon's dalmatic. Small trapezes, plainly decorated with geometric designs, were, in the Middle Ages, enhanced with eagles, griffins and even angelic candle-bearers and scenes from the Gospel. Each flap woven in gold and fringed, became splayed out and was furnished with metallic appliqué work and even little bells. The ends finally evolved into the shape of wide shovels loaded with stiffened embroideries and silken tassels.

It is not so long since the narrower forms have been restored (three to four inches wide) for the stoles and their endings. There is little or no decoration. The fringes are its finest ornament and, though they are not required, give the stole a graceful appearance. The only thing insisted upon is the cross in the middle: it should be kissed before the stole is put on.

The formula used by the priest when donning it for Mass indicates its principal symbolical meaning: "Restore to me, Lord, the garment of immortality which I lost through the prevarication of my first parent; and, unworthy that I am to approach your sacred Majesty, may I nevertheless merit eternal happiness."

A second symbol, that of innocence, is revealed by the words of the bishop when he invests the deacon with the stole on the day of his ordination: "Receive the stole, the sign of innocence, from the Lord's hand; be faithful to your ministry for, if necessary, God can easily increase the succour of his grace in you, he, who reigns for ever, world without end." The stole is always worn for the celebration of Mass and the administration of the sacraments and sacramentals, but only by officiants: bishop, priest and deacon. Thus, at pontifical Mass, the assistant priest and deacons at the throne, who are really not celebrants, are merely clad in the cope, for the first, and the dalmatic for the two others, without stole or maniple; the bishop himself only puts it on for the functions which require it or if he

presides in pontifical vestments, but not as a sign of jurisdiction. It has been mentioned that priests cross the stole
when they wear the alb and then fasten it round their
waists with a cincture; but, on many occasions, priests, if
they are clad in surplices, let the two hanging sections fall
down in front, just as bishops do; for instance, when they
preside at the obsequies and other funeral offices, to ad-
minister sacraments and sacramentals, to bless, etc. The
stole which they then use is called a *pastoral stole* and its
two hanging parts may be tied breast-high by a ribbon or
cord with tassels so that they may fall evenly on each side.

The diaconal stole, which the deacon receives at ordination, is also furnished with a fastening placed lower down
than that of the pastoral stole, for the same reason.

THE BROAD STOLE

What is known as the *broad stole* is one of the insignia
but without ornament and is worn by the deacon over his
stole for high Masses in penitential seasons. It is not really
a stole but a rolled-up chasuble worn as a bandolier, like
certain soldiers and policemen, who roll up their capes or
raincoats so that they may not get in the way; the deacon
naturally takes off the folded chasuble first before donning
the broad stole, since, in principle, it is one and the same
garment; this ancient custom signifies the readiness of the
servant on taking up his duties. It should be noted that the
ceremonial of Holy Week, published in 1955, orders priests
who are going to communion to wear a stole from the beginning of the Maundy Thursday high Mass. They should also
provide themselves with one if, when sick, they receive
holy communion in bed.

Lastly, the colour of stoles is not without interest. For
Mass they are the same colour as the celebrant's chasuble.
The stole for funeral offices is black. For the sacraments,
it is white and violet for baptism, white for confirmation,
the Eucharist and marriage, violet for the sacrament of

penance and extreme unction. For blessings and sacramentals it is white or violet, as the case may be. It is usually white for processions, but violet for penitential processions and red if some instrument of the Passion (a piece of the true cross, of the crown of thorns, a nail of the crucifixion) or martyrs' relics are carried.

CHAPTER XIV

PRIESTLY VESTMENTS

For the celebration of Mass the priest first puts on the linen vestments, common to all officiants, the amice, alb and cincture; then the insignia, the maniple and the stole, and lastly the chasuble; he then puts on the biretta.

This distinctive vestment, the chasuble, is conferred upon him during the ordination ceremony. The bishop commences the investiture by exchanging the diaconal stole which the new priest wears for the sacerdotal stole: he places it across the breast, saying, "Accept the Lord's yoke, for this yoke is sweet and its burden light." He then invests him with the chasuble whose back section remains folded on the shoulders, while adding, "Accept the sacerdotal vestment which represents charity; for God is powerful enough to increase it in your soul and thus perfect his work."

THE CHASUBLE

In the time of the Republic and at the beginning of the Empire, the specifically Roman *byrrhus* or *amictus* was the "covering" called *toga*, which derived from a word related to the verb *tegere*, to cover. It was a large segment of a circle in white wool nearly three yards in diameter. As the state attire inseparable from all acts of their public functions, this garment which was the Romans' national dress continued to be worn during the Empire period. But it was found to be too cumbersome, too heavy and difficult to wear gracefully. The service of a well-trained slave was necessary in order to arrange its cunningly contrived folds. From the beginning of the second century the *toga* was discarded by those who went into the country: the *pallium*, the *lacerna*, which is a coloured *pallium*, and especially the *paenula*, a large winter and travelling cloak complete with hood (*cucullus*), were all preferred to the *toga*. In the fourth century the *toga* was no longer more than a ceremonial garment used by senators in the official sessions of their rank.

The *paenula* was a wide round covering with a hole in the middle for the head. It covered the whole body from head to foot, and kept off the rain, fog and cold. In fine weather it was folded loosely across the shoulders. Might not this be the mantle which St Paul left behind him with his hosts on a hot day? He inquires about it in his second letter to his disciple Timothy (4. 9–13): "Make haste and come quickly to me—when thou comest, bring with thee the cloak which I left in Carpus' hands at Troas, the books too, and above all the rolls of parchment." "Perhaps Paul is feeling the cold in his prison," says Canon Osty, "or does he merely wish to recover a garment which he cannot replace owing to his modest resources?"

The *paenula* was called *planeta* in the fourth century and this term, whose etymology is obscure, is still used in Italy as in our liturgical books.

It was not until the seventh century that it was called chasuble, or rather *casula*, a little tent, small house or little room; the wearer seemed to be shut up in a tent since even his head was covered with a hood.

The authentic shape of the chasuble is that of an enveloping garment, that is, conical and in folds. The rubrics of the Roman Missal direct the deacon or acolyte to raise the chasuble at the moment of the elevation. This evidently refers to the material on the arms because the vestment is presumed to be ample and conical. Since the Romans them-

selves had shortened the material of the *paenula* about the
arms, in order to be less hampered, we need not be surprised if the chasuble, dignified by its sacred use, has also
been subject to changes. The *casula*, an ample mantle,
supple and noble, which generously enfolded its wearer,
gradually lost its simplicity and became laden with
luxurious ornaments. It was a vestment common to all
ministers at the altar; some used to leave it in the vestry,
others took it off to perform their functions; thus, during
Lent the sacred ministers who still wear the chasuble do
not confine themselves to lifting it up in front (as is prescribed by the ceremonial), but take it off in the sanctuary
itself, the subdeacon for reading the Epistle, the deacon
for chanting the Gospel and then assisting the celebrant.
These relics of the discipline once in force, "folded
chasubles" as they are called, will probably be finally sup-
pressed, since the new *Ordo* for Holy Week (1955) has
replaced them by the dalmatic and the black tunicle for
Good Friday and by the same vestments in white for
carrying the ciborium to the altar of repose on Maundy
Thursday; thus only now can it be said that the chasuble
is the liturgical vestment proper to the celebrant alone.

The chasuble underwent the strangest mutilations. As
early as the sixth century, Etienne Durant complains, it
was "so cut and of such a deformed pattern that if it
were compared to the ancient *casula*, whence it derives, it
would be no longer worthy of the name". To allow for the
weight of the rich cloth and ornamentation it was cut away
over the arms at an early date, it was shortened in front or
behind or even on both sides at once, it was cut to a point
or in the shape of a shield.

During the Renaissance the limit was reached: while
widened out towards the bottom in Spain, in France and
in Belgium the front facing was cut in the shape of a
violin case in order to leave the arms completely free, and
its rear facing designed as a rectangle became a large plank

on which a cross was placed. The sacred vestment had almost everywhere become an "ornament", and what an ornament! Stiffened with buckram, heavier than ever, without suppleness, the chasuble had acquired an extremely banal character, so Léon Bloy was not afraid to declare that it was as rich as it was ugly, exclaiming vigorously: "Who then will free the sanctuary from these stiff and ungraceful scapulars, which bear absolutely no resemblance to the simple and ample vestments which priests wore in other days?"

Fortunately in the mid-nineteenth century Dom Guéranger, the restorer of liturgy in France, revived the use of large chasubles in his abbey at Solesmes. Following his example, the Benedictines of other countries delivered their monasteries from the skimpy shapes. The movement grew and strengthened: the secular clergy and even bishops wore the new type publicly and the good tradition was adopted everywhere.

The decree of the Congregation of Rites of August 20th, 1957, no longer requires recourse to the Holy See for the making and use of vestments whose shape departs from accepted custom, as did the preceding decrees of 1863 and 1925. It decides "to leave to the prudent judgement of Ordinaries the decision to allow or disallow such vestments while having regard to particular local circumstances". The dioceses where the bishop has never forbidden these modifications and where he himself makes daily use of ample chasubles are therefore authorized to make and use them.

It should also be noted that in 1863 the Congregation of Rites was consulted about chasubles called "Gothic". This was a very badly chosen term, because it is "an Italian Renaissance word, an insulting word", says Louis Gillet, "which means uncouth, barbarous". Moreover, it is unacceptable as a qualification for the vestments of the "Gothic" period of the thirteenth, fourteenth and fifteenth centuries, since no special type of chasuble was produced at the time: it remained as it had been in the two preceding centuries. In 1925 the decree mentioned the "ancient" shape. This was far more correct. In 1957 the same Congregation uses the expression "vestments of primitive shape". We are therefore gradually going farther back into the most distant past, and our fine chasubles, wide-shaped, supple, light, do certainly recall the real *casula* of the fifth century.

There is no liturgical law prescribing the decoration of the chasuble. It may be left unadorned as was practically the general case until the twelfth century; after all, a fine material should be quite sufficient. Doubtless, a start was made by strengthening the hem of the neck and shoulders in order to prevent the material from tearing, and by concealing the stitching by braids or gilt threads, whence these two bands reminiscent of the ancient *claves* which came down from the shoulders to the end of the garment. They were intended to cover up the stitches when five or three narrow widths of material were used. When two widths were sufficient, there was only one band which was placed in the middle of the back. It is called a *colum* and this seems to be the simplest and finest decoration. Doubtless cross-sections were added to it, either to form a Latin cross, or to imitate the pallium around the neck, or to recall the hood which disappeared at an unknown period. Like the other liturgical vestments the chief merit of the chasuble lies in its outline, the richness of its folds, the beauty and suppleness of its silken material.

The use of the chasuble for celebrating Mass is obligatory, but, without mentioning folded chasubles again, there are occasions on which priests may wear it though they themselves are not celebrants. On Maundy Thursday, at the chrism Mass, sung by the bishop in his cathedral, twelve priests clad in chasubles join in the blessing of the oils. They are the pontiff's cooperators, recalling the ancient *presbyterium* who formerly accompanied the head of the diocese. On the occasion of the consecration of a church, priests, similarly vested in chasubles, are appointed to carry the bier or biers (if there is a considerable number of altars to be consecrated) holding the sacred relics. At Corpus Christi processions, the clergy may be dressed in their own vestments: tunicles, dalmatics, chasubles, each according to his rank. This was the former practice (which may still exist in certain countries), when the canons assisted their bishop in his pontifical capacity at a high Mass. The chapter dignitaries wore copes, the canon-priests wore chasubles, the canon-deacons and subdeacons dalmatics and tunicles.

THE COPE

.The original *paenula* was sewn up in front as our chasuble still is. But it evolved: it soon became opened up as far as the breast, then up to the collar, a band of material was left to tie the two edges together. The arab cloak is just like this: and this band of material, the morse, is still found on our ancient copes, but they are provided with clasps. Such, then, is the origin of the cope or *pluviale*, a semicircular rain cloak, always provided with a hood; it is still a sleeveless garment but is no longer put on over the head like a chasuble.

When the biretta came into use the hood was no longer needed as a head covering: it was either reduced in size or replaced by a small piece of material as a relic of the original. This ornament lost its triangular outline and assumed the shape of a shield, it then changed to the circular shape which may still be seen today. It even took the form of a little apron, clinging to the middle of the back. Some years ago the real hood came into its own again and has happily replaced the so-called ornamental hood.

While all the Mass vestments are blessed the cope is not; it is not solemnly given during ordination ceremonies, no symbolical meaning has been assigned to it. This vestment which is a ceremonial garb without any special significance may be worn by all members of the clergy from the merely tonsured up to the sovereign pontiff; that indicates the very different occasions on which it may be worn. The celebrant priest or bishop may don it for solemn offices other than that of the Mass, with or without a stole, for instance for Vespers, Lauds, funerals, processions, etc. The bishop may also wear it for the administration of sacraments, such as baptism and marriage, and when assisting at councils and gatherings of his rank. It is then the mark of his dignity. On the other hand the cope is also a vestment common to cantors and lower clerics. In several dioceses, the ministers (often children) who carry the episcopal insignia are clad in copes.

CHAPTER XV

EPISCOPAL VESTMENTS AND INSIGNIA

It is only natural that bishops, because of their great dignity, should have a special garment (or rather garments) distinguishing them from other churchmen and a right to honorary privileges and to insignia corresponding to their office. Careful distinction must be made between their outdoor dress, choir dress and pontifical dress. Unless the contrary is stated, what is here said of bishops applies also to patriarchs, primates, archbishops and bishops who are not cardinals.

OUTDOOR DRESS

Bishops' outdoor dress differs very little from that of priests. They wear a black cassock and a hat of the same colour. They may however be recognized by certain ornaments, for instance, the scarlet buttons and button-holes of their cassock. Moreover, they have a pectoral cross hanging on a chain: a violet sash with violet fringes; on the ring finger of their right hand they wear a ring adorned with a precious stone which may be set off with diamonds; their head is covered with a violet skull cap. Their black hat is decorated with a green cord and tassels. Despite appearances to the contrary this is the correct colour for bishops. In all countries, even if it is not the custom to wear a cassock out of doors, their stock is violet and distinguishes them from priests, who always wear a black one. The stock is a small piece of cloth which shows under the collar of the cassock. Lastly, on their black shoes, they may wear golden or silver gilt buckles. They usually confine themselves to silver buckles; their stockings are violet. Patriarchs and Nuncios wear a green and gold cord on their black hat, prelates who are not bishops a violet cord, mitred abbots a black cord. The tassels are always the same colour as the cord.

For ceremonies, the bishop wears a very wide unlined mantle of violet silk over the costume we have just described; it is fastened around the neck by violet ribbons.

CHOIR DRESS

A bishop puts on a violet cassock adorned with crimson silk when officiating or present at a liturgical ceremony; in 1952 the train of this cassock was abolished for all ecclesiastics, even for cardinals, by decree of the Sacred Congregation of Rites.

Their pectoral cross is then hung on a green and golden cord at the end of which is a tassel of the same colours; their violet silken sash has violet tassels. Nuncios have two golden tassels on their watered-silk sashes.

The other items of their vesture are the same as for their outdoor dress. They wear a violet biretta for head-covering; like all prelates, they wear a rochet with crimson facings.

This costume is completed by three different garments, the mantelletta, the mozzetta and the cappa. As is obvious from its name the mantelletta is a small mantle. It does not reach as far as the knees. It has no sleeves but merely two slits in the sides for arms. Since the rochet is a sign of jurisdiction, this mantelletta covers it completely, seeing that it is used by all dignitaries who have no jurisdiction. All titular bishops, the residential bishop himself when he leaves his diocese, all prelates who are not bishops are honoured by this costume.

The mozzetta is a small cape provided with a tiny hood and is fastened down the breast by a line of buttons. It allows the rochet to be seen and is consequently suited to the bishop in residence in his diocese, to the archbishop in his whole province and to the apostolic nuncio in the whole territory to which he is accredited. When the bishop wishes to occupy his cathedral stall, he puts on his mozzetta; he should also wear this garment at home. In provincial councils all bishops wear the mozzetta because they share in the metropolitan archbishop's jurisdiction.

The cappa is a large formal mantle, furnished with a long train which is held up by a cleric called train-bearer. Since 1952 the Sacred Congregation of Rites has ordered the shortening of this train while permitting the use of the ancient cappa. It is always violet coloured even when the bishop wears a black cassock; we shall mention later in what circumstances. His large hood is lined with violet; it is of ermine in winter and red silk in summer.

The cappa with the train is a sign of jurisdiction. As in the case of the mozzetta the following are entitled to wear it: the bishop residing in his diocese, the metropolitan in his province and the apostolic nuncio in the territory to which he is accredited. This vestment is on a par with the throne; therefore, if a bishop from outside the diocese has been allowed to use the throne to perform a pontifical function he may come wearing the cappa. On the other hand, the folded cappa, that is, with the train carried across the left arm by the prelate himself, is correct for all bishops when they attend solemn ceremonies in the Sovereign Pontiff's presence or that of the Sacred College, for the local bishop in presence of a cardinal or of the metropolitan and for coadjutor or auxiliary bishops if they have the permission of the diocesan bishop.

The following changes are made in choir dress during

penitential seasons (Advent, Lent, Ember Days, etc.) and at all funeral offices: the bishop's cassock, mantelletta and mozzetta are black and adorned with violet silk; the sash and its tassels are black; the rochet, preferably without lace, has violet trimmings. The biretta and skull cap are violet for all seasons. At Rome the bishops wear a violet costume on all occasions because of the pope's presence which calls for a special etiquette and solemnity. Outside Rome the wearing of this mourning attire was formerly obligatory at stated ceremonies and days but in our time the contrary custom has prevailed and bishops only use black for Good Friday and when the Holy See is vacant.

We have already mentioned two episcopal insignia which are only worn by the bishop from the day of his consecration, namely, the pectoral cross and the ring.

It was owing to a change of discipline that the pectoral cross became an episcopal privilege. In the early centuries Christians hung some sacred token around their neck: a tablet inscribed with a Gospel text; a medal with the sign of the cross or Christ's initials, such as Geneviève received from the holy bishop St Germanus of Auxerre; a small custodial containing fragments stained with the blood of martyrs or relics of saints (*encolpium*), sometimes even the Holy Eucharist.

This is the sole origin of the pectoral cross. The faithful abandoned this practice while pastors devoutly continued it. In their case it is rather a traditional devotion than one of the real insignia. They are not invested with this cross during the consecration ceremony and it is not blessed, it does not betoken jurisdiction since all bishops may wear it everywhere and, lastly, it does not come under the heading of those objects which cardinals and bishops are obliged to bequeath to the pontifical treasury or to their cathedral. In the west it is a Latin cross and made of gold or gilt silver. It contains the relics of martyrs or other saints, as is proved by the short prayer which the prelate recites when putting it around his neck. Protonotaries apostolic, who are prelates without episcopal functions, are the only ones who cannot wear the pectoral cross at all times: they only put it on when celebrating pontifically as they are authorized to do.

The ring is one of the real episcopal insignia which the kneeling candidate receives during his consecration. Having blessed it, the consecrator puts it on the fourth finger of the candidate's right hand, saying: "Accept this ring as a token of the inviolable faithfulness with which you should protect the Bride of God, that is, the Church." This formula explains all the symbolism of the ring; it is "the token of the union contracted between the new pastor and his Church, of the union which our Saviour himself, present and acting in the bishop, has contracted with his bride, the universal Church", said Dom Gréa. The ring, token of the faithfulness which the parties vow to each other, is in fact the symbol of the alliance.

The shape of the ring represents eternity, or at least perpetuity, duration. It also evokes the link of the chain which binds the bishop closely to his local Church. Lastly, the word *signaculum*, which the consecrator pronounces, indicates the origin of the ring as a seal, and a sign of authority and power. The bishop is trustee of heavenly gifts, he must keep secret the secret things and reveal what should be known. Possessing a definite mark of identity he seals official documents, and is empowered to authenticate all acts consigned to writing. He must bind what should be bound and loose what should be loosed.

The episcopal ring is made of gold symbolizing charity and adorned with a precious stone which may be offset with diamonds. This stone may be of any colour, except sapphire, which is reserved for cardinals. No design is engraved upon it.

Besides the ring which they use in everyday life and for ordinary ceremonies, bishops have a pontifical ring when

they officiate in a solemn manner. It should be slightly
larger in diameter so that it may be worn over the glove.
Regular abbots, from the time of their blessing by the
bishop, also wear a ring with a stone, but without any
diamonds.

With the exception of the skull cap and the biretta which
are always violet, the dress of religious who have been
promoted to the rank of bishop differs from the one we
have just described. This applies solely to those religious
who belong to the great monastic orders (the others follow
the general rule): they keep the colour of their religious
habit for their choir and outdoor attire, without any violet
ornaments. Thus, for Benedictines the costume is all black,
white for the Camaldolese and the Premonstratensians,
cinder for the Franciscans, brown for the Capuchins. The
Cistercians and the Carthusians wear a white cassock,
black mantelletta and mozzetta and a black cappa with a
white hood. The Dominicans are similarly dressed but their
mantelletta and mozzetta are trimmed with white and the
cappa is all white.

PONTIFICAL DRESS

When the diocesan bishop comes to his cathedral or to
a church in his diocese to celebrate a high Mass (which is
called *pontifical Mass*) he is clad in choir dress, that is,
he wears the cappa. He is already shod in liturgical sandals
whose colour corresponds to the day's Mass. As he reaches
his throne he takes off his cappa, puts the biretta on his
head and washes his hands. Then, with the assistance of
the deacon and subdeacon, he successively dons the amice,
alb, cincture, pectoral cross, stole, tunicle, dalmatic, gloves,
chasuble, mitre and lastly the ring which the assistant priest
places on his finger. Before going to the altar he is given
the crozier which he holds in his left hand.

Having said the opening prayers at the foot of the altar,
the maniple is placed on his left arm. With the exception

of the tunicle, dalmatic, gloves, mitre and cross, we have already described these other vestments and insignia in their proper place. The tunicle and the dalmatic are a smaller form of the tunicle and dalmatic worn by the sub-deacon and deacon. This, in fact, is intended to show that the bishop possesses the fullness of the priesthood and consequently all the orders which he confers upon clerics, and he thus wears together the vestments proper to the three sacred orders, in the sequence of their reception at ordinations, namely the tunicle, dalmatic and chasuble. These tunicles (the current name applied to the first two) are made of light silk material, in one piece and unlined so that they may not be too cumbersome for the prelate; they should be shaped differently, the tunicle shorter than the dalmatic with longer and narrower sleeves. They are decorated with gold braid.

The gloves, whose real liturgical name is *chirothecae* (covering for the hands), are made of silk and of the same colour as the other vestments, just like the tunicles; it is forbidden, however, to wear black gloves for funeral ceremonies. The episcopal glove has a special shape: a kind of cuff called gauntlet, guard, wristband or frill covers the wrist and the edge of the sleeve of the alb. It is embroidered; the back of the glove itself is ornamented with golden thread or golden embroidery, representing Christ's initials or a Greek cross. The general purpose of gloves is that of a protective covering for the hands and especially for priestly hands which perform the august mysteries of the altar and which serve as the instrument of other acts of the sacred ministry. At a first glance they are not therefore special to the episcopate; they were merely confined to it by privilege since the eleventh century; they are referred to in several ancient documents from the sixth century onwards.

Thus, Hildebert, bishop of Meaux (672–760), in the legend, takes his gloves off for the consecration and hangs them on a sunbeam. In the sacramentary of Ratoldus, abbot of Corbie, who died in 986, we read that the prelate, having washed his hands before celebrating the holy sacrifice, received the gloves and said a special prayer while putting them on. After the offertory, he returned to the throne and took them off to wash his hands again.

Mgr de Conny, one of the foremost French liturgists of the nineteenth century, states that "according to the etiquette on which the Church's traditions are founded, bare hands denote respect; no one dared to approach a superior and serve him with gloved hands—even today one must remove one's gloves for an audience with the pope". We should not be surprised by the fact that the use of gloves is forbidden in church by a rule to which there is no exception except for bishops and even then only on a special and very definite occasion.

This is only at the solemn Mass celebrated by the bishop himself, but not at the Mass for the dead. Neither does he wear them when he merely assists at Mass. Besides, at the offertory, before he offers up the bread, the prelate takes off his gloves and washes his hands. He does not put them on again until after the last Gospel, except when he is imparting the papal blessing. The bishop's ministers, even when they are canons, are not entitled to wear them and still less the serving clerics, train-bearers, etc., seminarists and choir-boys, under any pretext whatever.

The *Ceremonial of Bishops* debars the crozier-bearer from using gloves. He must grasp it with the sleeve of his surplice or the ends of a scarf.

The prohibition of the wearing of gloves by the faithful in certain circumstances should therefore be rigorously enforced for it is easily justified. When they receive a sacrament or a sacramental, for instance, ashes, the Candlemas candle or the palm on Palm Sunday; when they act as godfather or godmother, at baptism or confirmation; when they are honoured by carrying the canopy for the Blessed

Sacrament. We read in *Le parfait ecclésiastique*, a work published in 1665 by Claude de la Croix, a priest of the Saint-Nicolas-du-Chardonnet seminary at Paris: "The laity must be warned that they should neither wear gloves on their hands nor masks on their face when they go to Mass, confession, holy communion, kiss holy relics, kiss the cross on Good Friday, receive ashes on their heads, take holy water, have the holy Gospel said over them and such-like acts of religion, where every Christian conducts himself as modestly and humbly as he can."

The bishop's *chirothecae* are all the more worthy of our respect since they are blessed during the course of the consecration ceremony itself by the officiant who afterwards gives them to the bishop-elect who kneels before him.

Whether he is vested in the chasuble for Mass or wears the cappa for the other pontifical functions, the bishop wears the mitre on his head. It is the ceremonial headpiece for prelates: it is made of two triangular sections sewn down the sides and held together by a lining which is wide enough to allow the necessary opening for the head; two small fringed bands of the same material and colour (the *fanons*), are attached to the back end of the mitre.

The mitre and the tiara seem to have the same origin. Modern authors disagree about them: some date them back to very ancient times while others bring their institution forward to about the eleventh century.

The high priest of the Mosaic religion certainly wore a golden band on his forehead and it is also said that the apostles St James and St John did likewise. Tertullian († c. 220), in his treatise *De Corona*, refers to *crowned* apostles, evangelists and bishops. Other writers refer to a sacerdotal crown, a crown of glory. When the tomb of St Cuthbert, bishop of Lindisfarne († 687), was opened a golden band was found around his forehead. About the eleventh century bishops are represented in iconography decked out in a kind of Phrygian bonnet tied around their head by a cord whose ends fall down at the back.

Dom Leclercq believes that this mitre is a variant of the ancient *corona*. In order to avoid contact with the metal a band of cloth was placed underneath it, and the metal band was later replaced by a golden braid. This headband which has the special shape of a diadem is the principal distinguishing mark of the *mitra*, a Latin term which originally referred to the narrow bands which encircled the head.

In the twelfth century a round-shaped projection appeared on each side of the episcopal head-covering and, in the following century, these were placed at the front and back as they still are today.

On the other hand the narrow bands which kept the covering down on the head and were tied behind no longer consisted of a piece of cloth distinct from the headpiece. They, in turn, were replaced by a rich braid forming the lower border of the mitre and by two fanons attached to it.

According to the symbolism adopted by the Roman Pontifical the mitre is a protective helmet whose purpose is to render the new pontiff formidable to the enemies of truth, and it prescribes the following formula for the consecrator at the very moment when he places the mitre on the new bishop: "We place this helmet of protection and salvation, O Lord, on the head of this bishop, your soldier, so that his face which will be ornamented with it and his head armed with it, as with the horns of the two Testaments, may appear terrible to the enemies of truth and so that he may become their powerful adversary, through your grace, you whose word caused the face of Moses to shine forth by illuminating it with the shining horns of the magnificence of your truth, you who ordered a tiara to be placed on the head of Aaron, your pontiff."

Bishops have three different mitres; the precious mitre, usually of golden cloth embellished with embroidery and precious stones, is used for the most solemn functions, for the second half of Mass and of pontifical Vespers. The gold mitre in white silk with golden embroidery and without pearls, is used for administering the sacraments and for the first half of Mass and pontifical Vespers. The plain mitre, of white linen, has a lining of the same colour (instead of red) and its fanons have red fringes at their ends. The pontiff puts it on for penitential days, on Good Friday and for all funeral offices.

The bishop wears the mitre whenever he moves about or sits, gives his solemn blessing, is censed, or washes his hands.

The crozier is not only a distinguishing mark of the episcopate but also a sign of jurisdiction. Indeed the bishop does not use it outside his diocese unless obliged to do so by the nature of the function he celebrates, such as ordinations, dedication of a church, etc.[1] In liturgical books it is always called the pastoral staff, which clearly indicates its symbolism. It is at one and the same time a ruling staff, a royal sceptre and the shepherd's crook with which the pastor assembles and leads his flock and, if need be, punishes the recalcitrant. Moreover it has a point at its lower end which allows him to spur on the weak and raise them up, and to use it as a defensive arm against the church's enemies. The crozier is also a support. The bishop holds it in his hands during the singing of the Gospel, as if to lean on it. This is an episcopal privilege since, according to ancient liturgical documents, the assistants, clergy and faithful alike, all had to lay down the staffs, on which they were leaning, at this moment.

The primitive shape of the crozier was straight or slightly bent at the top. It finished in a knot, or sometimes a crystal ball. About the eleventh century the curve was changed into a richly wrought volute which was later decorated with allegorical figures. The wood was replaced by gilt or

[1] When several bishops are present together only one should carry the crozier.

silvered metal or simply sheathed in copper as is often the case in our time. For some years now the former wood and ivory have come back into use for the decoration of the crozier and give it a very artistic finish.

The crozier is not normally used apart from the mitre; these two are co-related insignia, as is stated in the *Ceremonial of Bishops*. There are, however, exceptions to this rule: while the Gospel or a Gospel canticle, such as the *Magnificat* of Vespers, is being sung the pontiff bares his head as a sign of respect and also during funeral offices which do not call for the use of the crozier. The latter is particularly suitable for processions and for all pontifical acts which are performed by the bishop himself: he carries it in his left hand and always turns the crook towards the congregation. He grasps it in his right hand on one occasion only, that is, when he traces the Greek and Latin letters on the scattered ashes during the consecration of a church.

When the bishop is clad in a chasuble or a cappa, four clerics are appointed to carry his insignia. The *Ceremonial of Bishops* mentions them first of all among the servers and allows them to wear the cope in ceremonies where the chapter canons are themselves vested. Since the bishop is the only one to use the mitre and the crozier the two clerics who have charge of these objects serve no other purpose than that of holding them at such times as the bishop does not require them during ceremonies where he uses them. Now, he does not use them when he wishes but only when he is vested. In the circumstances, therefore, these objects are laid aside when they are not being used for some time. Consequently, the mitre and crozier are not required for the procession of the bishop or archbishop on his way to his cathedral; if he should be vested for the ceremony to which he is going, they will be laid near the altar beforehand, together with the other vestments; if vestments are not called for, they need only remain in their cases.

The significance of the books and the hand-candle must

also be mentioned. We purposely speak of books in the plural; they are a Gospel book, a Canon, a Breviary, an Antiphonary, a Pontifical, respectively, according to the nature and requirements of the function. Granted that the use of the Pontifical and Canon is proper to bishops, a book, whatever its kind, is merely a useful object, without any special significance, which the officiant never takes in his hands; it cannot be rightly included among episcopal insignia.

As regards the hand-candle, although its use is truly episcopal and it has been given a very special shape for convenience, namely, a low frame with a long handle, it can only be looked upon as an accessory to the books, and dependent on them for its function, since it is meant to give light, both in a literal and figurative sense, to the bishop who is reading them. The rôle of this candlestick cannot be compared to those carried by the acolytes which are a sign of honour and derive from a more ancient rite; it is merely intended to go with the book, to be used with it where and when it is needed. Apart from that, books and candlesticks are only an encumbrance.

The mitre-bearer and the crozier-bearer have their shoulders covered with a veil or scarf of the same colour as the vestments. For funeral offices the mitre-bearer's scarf is violet and there is no crozier-bearer. Each bearer holds his insigne with the folds of this scarf.

The four bearers always walk behind the bishop when he goes from place to place. The crozier-bearer alone carries the insignia assigned to him immediately in front of the pontiff when the latter cannot take it himself, for instance, in processions when he is carrying the monstrance. In the procession of palms he walks behind the bishop. In this case the cleric, who then ceases to be a mere carrier, becomes so to speak the delegated bearer of the crozier.

CHAPTER XVI

ARCHIEPISCOPAL INSIGNIA

The title of Patriarch or Primate implies no special jurisdiction but merely a prerogative of honour and a right of
precedence over all the other bishops. These high dignitaries have no particular emblems.

A metropolis (mother-town) is the town which is—or has
been—the most important in a region. The Church is thus
divided into ecclesiastical provinces made up of several
dioceses. A metropolitan or archbishop resides in the
metropolis of each of them and has the same responsibilities and the same rights in his diocese as other bishops
have in theirs.

Two honorary distinctions are attached to the archiepiscopal rank: the use of the pallium and the privilege
enjoyed by archbishops of having the cross borne in front
of them. In exceptional cases certain bishops, it is true,
enjoy this double privilege or merely the first, either as a
personal right or because of a perpetual concession granted
to their see.

The two emblems have this in common, that they
emanate from the apostolic see as the symbol of a fuller
participation in the dignity and power vested in the
supreme pontificate.

The pallium is a plain band of cloth which is worn on

the shoulders and breast like a collar. Its origin is obscure: it was originally perhaps a real mantle (the *pallium* of Greek and Roman women) as its name would lead us to believe or else the *lorum*, a scarf which Romans wore around their necks on special occasions, or even an imperial ornament which the Head of the Church had inherited. Or possibly we should attribute its institution to St Linus, Peter's first successor, according to a tradition contained in the Ceremonial of Augustine Patrizzi (1488). The fact remains that its use in Rome may have been borrowed from the Greek metropolitans and bishops who already wore it by right at the Council of Nicea (325). The oldest reference to the pallium as a liturgical ornament is found in a notice about the pope St Mark (in *Liber pontificalis* composed in the sixth century), who is said to have given it to the bishop of Ostia; in representations seen at Rome and Ravenna, which date from the sixth and seventh centuries, this emblem appears larger than it now is and its two bands start from the left shoulder and come down to the lower part of the body in front and behind. This custom was still in force up to the tenth century.

As regards the material of the pallium, St Isidore of Pelusium has clearly pointed out its symbolism: "The *homophorion*" (which is its Greek name), he says, "made of wool and not of linen, symbolizes the skin of that sheep which the Lord sought when it was lost and which he brought back on his shoulders. Now, the bishop, who represents Christ, fulfils the same office and shows everyone by his dress that he is the imitator of this good and great pastor who took upon himself the infirmities of his flock." At Rome, in the basilica of St Agnes-without-the-walls, on the via Nomentana, which is dedicated to this martyr saint, two white lambs are blessed by the abbot of the Canons Regular of the Lateran, on her feast, January 21st, after he has sung pontifical Mass. They are then presented to the Sovereign Pontiff, who blesses them again from his palace window. They are then given into the care of the Benedictines of St Cecilia in the Trastevere who must feed and shear them. Their fleece is used to make the palliums which are blessed by the pope or a bishop on June 28th in the Vatican basilica. On the vigil of the feast of Saints Peter and Paul these insignia are laid on their tombs for a night. Only then are they handed over to the prelate appointed to keep them carefully and to give them to those for whom they are intended.

The privilege of wearing the pallium has become a right for metropolitans (not for titular archbishops) who must send a written request to the Holy Father in order to obtain it. If the interested party is going to Rome the first cardinal deacon invests him with it, if on the other hand he cannot travel to the eternal city, a pontifical delegate is commissioned to deliver it to him during a very special ceremony, which is found in the Roman Pontifical. The delegated bishop celebrates pontifical Mass, then, seated at the faldstool at the foot of the altar, he receives the elect's oath of fidelity on behalf of the apostolic see. The new archbishop, vested as for pontifical Mass, except for mitre and gloves, then receives the pallium on his shoulders. The archiepiscopal cross, of which we shall speak later on, is presented to him for the first time and the metropolitan, standing before it bareheaded, and with his back to the altar, imparts his solemn blessing to the congregation.

The Church attaches such importance to the giving of this insigne that before receiving it patriarchs, primates and archbishops cannot bear their title, consecrate bishops, call a council, consecrate the holy chrism, consecrate a church nor ordain clerics. On the other hand, an archbishop cannot use his predecessor's pallium and, even when transferred from one see to another, use that which he has already received from the Holy See.

It is the archdeacon of the Roman Church who places the pallium on the Sovereign Pontiff's shoulders on the day of his coronation. The pope may naturally wear it everywhere since he rules the whole world. Other dignitaries who have received the privilege may only wear it in their province (or in their diocese) solely at pontifical Mass and on the days decreed in the Pontifical.

The archiepiscopal cross is the second emblem attaching to the rank of archbishop. The privilege of having a cross borne before them is a reflection of the apostolate of the supreme head of the Church. Indeed, the Sovereign Pontiff is always preceded by a processional cross to show that he brings the revelation of the mystery of the Cross to the whole world. Now, among the missionaries associated with his apostolate, the most distinguished are those of the earliest centuries who made their way towards the cities of the Roman provinces and established their sees therein.

The cross which is carried before their successors in our own day should thus remind each country of the evangelization whose benefits are due to the bishop of Rome. Did not Pope Silvester II, in letters of March 27th in the year 1000, grant St Stephen, king of Hungary, the privilege (which was to descend to his successors) of having the cross borne before him? This was because of his apostolic zeal, since this honour is the emblem of the apostolate, *apostolatus insigne*.

The *Ceremonial of Bishops* states in several places that the figure on the crucifix should be turned towards the archbishop. Thus, when he enters his province for the first time "he has the cross carried by one of his chaplains, the image of the crucified Lord being turned towards him". This is done constantly to show him that Jesus Christ crucified is the object of his apostolate. Though he enjoys this privilege throughout his entire province it should nevertheless be noted that he must forgo it in the presence of a higher ecclesiastic. The cross is carried immediately before his person. Only canons may walk between it and the archbishop; in other words the archiepiscopal cross may serve at the same time as the cross for the cathedral chapter.

CHAPTER XVII

CARDINALS' VESTMENTS AND INSIGNIA

The special clothing (which no other church dignitary is allowed to wear) of the members of the Sacred College, who constitute the Roman Pontiff's senate, takes its origin from their very high dignity.

Scarlet is the colour reserved for them. Thus, even their outdoor costume, which includes a black cassock, is ornamented with red buttons and button-holes, with a watered silk sash and fringes of the same colour. Their ceremonial cloak and their stock are also red; the cord and tassels of their black hat are red; their black shoes are edged with red piping and furnished with gold buckles. They also have a red hat edged with golden braids for officiating at very solemn ceremonies. The Princes of the Church receive what is called the cardinal's hat from the pope's hands at the consistory. It is made of red cloth with a very wide brim and ornamented with thirty red tufts, fifteen on each side; the cords were formerly used to tie the headpiece under the chin. The cardinals never actually wear this big hat: it is exhibited at their home, and at their death it is placed at their lying-in-state. At their funeral a servant has the honour of carrying it behind the hearse; lastly, it is hung on the vault of the cathedral, if the deceased is a resident bishop or archbishop. It is when conferring it on the new cardinals that the pope explains the symbolism of its red colour and consequently that of all the cardinals' garments, reminding them of their duty to defend the rights of holy Church even to the point of shedding their blood for her sake. On the coat of arms the hat has retained its character as an insigne: it surmounts the shield and its tassels hang down on each side.

Boniface VIII (1294) conferred the red cassock, as a choir dress, on cardinals. Paul II (1464) granted them the hat and skull cap of the same colour, the purple mantle and the scarlet hose when they rode on horseback. The cardinal wears a sash of red watered silk with two golden tassels on this cassock, a rochet with red trimmings, the red mozzetta and the pectoral cross hung on a red and golden cord. As already stated, the skull cap, stock and stockings are red. The biretta, of the same colour, is made of cloth for winter and of watered silk for summer wear.

Cardinals may officiate from the diocesan bishop's throne in all churches throughout the world. They then put on the red cappa with train held by a train-bearer. No other throne may be raised when a cardinal is present. If there are several of them, they take their places under a baldacchinum as members of the same college, the foremost of all, the Sacred College. The diocesan, if he himself is vested in the cardinal's purple, occupies the last place in deference to his colleagues. The winter cappa is made of red silk lined with ermine and without tails. As a matter of fact, silk is specially reserved for cardinals and for all who are attached to the pontifical court, just as velvet is confined to the pope. The members of the Sacred College use watered silk as apostolic nuncios do. For penitential times and funeral offices the cassock, mozzetta and cappa are violet.

At Rome, the dignity of the cardinals is, so to speak, veiled out of respect for the Sovereign Pontiff's presence: the train of the cappa is never borne, they generally wear the mantelletta, and, when the pope is present, the mozzetta over this last garment. Nobody carries the crozier since the sovereign pontiff does not use this emblem. Lastly, the cardinals wear a cappa of violet wool with a similar hood, on Good Friday. Religious of the principal orders who have been promoted to the rank of cardinal keep the particular colour of their order; they nevertheless have a red skull cap and red biretta.

As regards pontifical dress there is nothing to distinguish the cardinals from bishops. When celebrating in a pontifical capacity they wear all the liturgical vestments and have the same insignia as residential bishops. As in the case of the latter they are accorded all the liturgical honours, with the single exception of the use of the seventh candlestick of the pontifical Mass (which is the strict privilege of the bishop in his diocese), and of the bearing of the archiepiscopal cross before them, which is confined to the metropolitan.

CHAPTER XVIII

THE SOVEREIGN PONTIFF'S VESTMENTS AND INSIGNIA

All pilgrims who have had the honour of being received in audience by the Sovereign Pontiff have seen him dressed in a white woollen or white silk cassock with a watered silk sash provided with fringes of golden tassels, and with a plain white skull cap as headgear. This is the pope's usual attire when inside his apartments. For more solemn audiences he puts on a rochet of fine linen inset with lace and a small red velvet cape, fringed with ermine in winter and with scarlet satin in summer. Purple, which popes inherited from the Roman emperors, is their special colour. When he leaves his apartments the pope also wears a red stole; his shoes are made of velvet cloth or red wool and their uppers are ornamented with a cross embroidered in gold.

The pious eastern custom of kissing sovereigns' feet seems to date back to the apostolic age; it has been said that St Clement kissed St Peter's, that the Emperor Constantine kissed those of St Silvester, the Emperor Justin those of John I. The Lombard kings imitated these examples which Italian princes have always followed.

History, indeed, teaches us that Charlemagne went up

the steps of St Peter's basilica on his knees while kissing each step successively and that he lowered his victorious head before Pope Adrian, and kissed the Pontiff's feet respectfully as a token of homage.

Popes refer the honour which they thus receive to God since it is the sign of the redemption which is represented on their shoes as on most of their liturgical vestments and on their insignia. The authority vested in them derives from the Cross.

When he leaves his palace, even if he merely goes into the Vatican gardens, the pope puts on a felt hat turned up at the sides, covered with a cloth of red silk, edged with golden braid and encircled with a cord hung with golden tassels.

Most of his ceremonial vestments are those common to bishops. Besides the tiara there are three which are always reserved for him exclusively: the *falda*, the *fanon* and the *subcinctorium*.

When he is not himself officiating, if, for instance, he is attending papal chapels in the presence of cardinals, patriarchs, archbishops, bishops and prelates of the pontifical court, the pope first dons the *falda* then the rochet, the amice, the alb, the cincture, the stole, the cappa with train, ornamented with a precious design, and lastly the mitre.

The *falda* is a long wide white silken skirt with an extremely ample train which falls around the feet on all sides; when walking the Sovereign Pontiff is accompanied by ecclesiastical dignitaries who raise and hold the front and back of this robe. The train itself is borne by the Prince Assistant at the throne. This curious ornament is referred to in relation to St Pius V's accession in 1566. Its use is thought to date farther back but it is as difficult to be precise about the period when the popes took to wearing it as it is to define its mystical meaning.

The use of the pontifical ring dates back to much earlier

times: St Stephen I, elected pope in 254, already used a special ring when fulfilling his sacred functions. The Sovereign Pontiff not only habitually wears a golden ring with a cameo of precious stones, but he uses a ring called pontifical for religious ceremonies. This is richer than that of bishops and its stone is often engraved.

Cardinal's or bishop's stones are not usually given to him (amethyst, sapphire, topaz or ruby) but there is obviously no rule governing his rings: he selects freely from amongst those which are offered to him.

The Fisherman's ring, proper to the Sovereign Pontiff, is so called because it bears the image of the apostle St Peter in a boat, casting or drawing his nets into or from the sea. It is a personal ring and the name of the reigning pontiff is engraved upon it. Its use is confined to the sealing of certain official documents, such as briefs coming from the apostolic secretariat. Since the time of Leo X, in 1521, the principal master of ceremonies in the presence of the cardinals breaks this ring on the occasion of the pope's death; this evidently symbolizes the ending of the juris-diction.

When celebrating pontifical Mass the pope, in addition to the vestments and insignia already mentioned, uses the pectoral cross, the tunicles, the chasuble instead of the cope, the fanon, the *subcinctorium*, the gloves and the pallium.

The fanon, an emblem special to the supreme pontiff, dates back, perhaps, to the twelfth century. It is a silk-lined cloak or rather two superimposed mozzettas, orna-mented with white and gold stripes, joined together by a purple cord; a shining cross is embroidered on the breast and the cardinal-deacon kisses it when placing this emblem on the pope's shoulders. The latter puts it on after the pectoral cross over the alb, the second half is lifted up and covers his head until he has put on his other vestments; it finally comes down over the chasuble like a cape.

The *subcinctorium* takes the form of a maniple hung on the side of the cincture of the alb.

The pope's pallium is the same as that of archbishops. After the prayers said at the foot of the altar the pontiff first receives the maniple (like all bishops) from the hands of the kneeling subdeacon, then the pallium which the two cardinal-deacons lay upon his shoulders.

The pope uses three different mitres for various occasions: the *glorious*, decorated with jewels and a circle of gold which forms its base; the *second*, equally rich but devoid of this circle; the *third*, of silver cloth for funeral offices and penitential seasons.

The tiara sometimes replaces the mitre. It has the same origin: a conical headpiece laid over a crown. The word appeared for the first time in the biography of Paschal II in the *Liber pontificalis* (1118). It had previously been called *regnum*. At the beginning of the fourteenth century, this headgear became larger and was richly ornamented with precious stones and two rear fanons. The upper portion soon ended in a golden globe and a second crown was added. One of the Avignon popes placed a third crown upon it and called it *triregnum*.

This superimposition of three crowns symbolizes the imperial power, the royal power and the sacerdotal power. "They remind the faithful", wrote the chevalier Moroni in the last century, "of the power wielded by the vicar of Jesus Christ in the Church militant and suffering, and even in the Church triumphant, owing to the privilege he has of decreeing the public veneration of God's servants who have merited the honour of canonization."

We have made no reference to the crozier for the very good reason that the pope does not use one.

Doubtless, he formerly used one or at least he received, when coming to the throne, an uncurved baton, or *ferula*, an emblem of government and of correction (from *ferio*, I strike): this custom survived until the sixteenth century and then fell into disuse. Serious authors had maintained that the curve of the crozier signified a limitation of power and that it was not suited to be placed in the hands of the universal pastor.

The *ferula*, currently used by the pope, is a cross without a crucifix. It is employed on all occasions when the liturgical function calls for the use of the crozier, for instance, the consecration of bishops, ordinations, etc.

On the other hand, he has a cross in gilt silver, which differs in no way from other processional crosses, carried before him. As is the case with residential archbishops, the image of the crucified Lord is always turned towards him and he imparts his blessing without wearing a mitre when he wears pontifical dress.

Under certain conditions, which occur infrequently nowadays, the pontiff gives his blessing with his tiara on his head, but away from the throne and altar. The cross in such circumstances, instead of being carried before him, remains in its place in the procession. It should be noted that this papal cross has only one cross-section. The double-branched cross, used in the east from time immemorial, is only seen on archbishops' coats of arms and similarly the cross with three branches has never appeared on the papal arms except as a result of artists' ignorance.

The first thing to be noted among the pope's prerogatives is the *Sedia gestatoria* which is nothing other than the pontifical faldstool of crimson velvet emblazoned with the arms of the reigning pope and placed on a horizontal support borne on the shoulders of the pontifical grooms. It is evidently a mark of supreme honour in imitation of the custom, formerly so widespread, of raising up on a shield the person who had been recognized by the people as their king.

The *flabella*, which resemble large fans made of peacocks' feathers, are fixed on the right and left of the *sedia*, and lend it a very imposing appearance for solemn processions. These emblems, which are still used in Africa and the east for high dignitaries, remind us of a practice which was very common among the Romans. During sacrifices and meals the *flabella*-bearers waved these fans of various shapes in order to chase away insects and freshen the air. *Flabella* are still used today in several oriental rites during the celebration of the liturgy, but they cannot be entirely likened to those which constitute a token of distinction reserved for the pope.

In the Byzantine rite especially this instrument, called *rhipidion*, has turned into a metal disk fixed on an arm or little wooden or metal pole.

An image of a six-winged seraph is engraved in mezzo-relievo on the disk. The deacon waves the *rhipidion* over the sacred species at certain moments during the Mass, particularly during pontifical Mass, as a symbol of the trembling of the wings of the seraphim who surround our Saviour. There are also usually two or several *rhipidia* to accompany the person carrying the cross in processions.

One should see the pontifical procession passing by at Saint Peter's for nearly two hours like a glistening ribbon, with the representatives of the monastic orders, the canons, the chamberlains with cloak and sword, the auditors of the Rota, the penitentiaries, the white-mitred bishops, the long scarlet stream of cardinals. Finally the silver trumpets blare out, thunderous applause bursts forth at the threshold of the basilica; a ray of sunshine falls obliquely from the cupola upon the pope, with the tiara on his head, wrapped in a wide golden cape, who stands out, pale with emotion, against the high red back of the *sedia gestatoria* which is slowly weaving its way, on the shoulders of twenty *sediari* in liveries of brocade, towards the confessional altar where eighty-nine perpetual lamps shine around the tomb of St Peter.

For a better understanding of this magnificence we should re-read the texts composed in honour of the priesthood by Ben Sira, author of Ecclesiasticus, who was very deeply impressed by the beauty of the High Priest's vestments, "nor sun ever shed on our temple such generous rays as he", rays which sparkle with the reflected light of the sacred vestments. Ben Sira sees in this the symbol of the glory of God in his temple.

> Such was he when he put on his robes of office, clad himself with the full majesty of array, sacred garments in which he went up to the sacred altar.
>
> There he stood, by the altar, with the priests handing him their portions, every one for sacrifice; and all these standing about him were but Lebanon cedars standing about Lebanon, were but as palm branches growing from their parent stem, all these sons of Aaron in the splendour of their attire. . . .
>
> Loud shouted the sons of Aaron, loud the silver trumpets blew; great was the cry raised to win God's audience. The singers, too, broke into chants of praise; sweetly their voices echoed through the wide courts; nor would the people leave off their praying to the Lord . . . till the divine praise was completed. And then Simon would come down, his hand outstretched over the assembly of Israel, a blessing on his lips . . . for the better manifestation of God's power. (Ecclus. 50. 5–20.)

Thus, the priestly vesture is magnificent and resplendent, not only for the purpose of honouring the pope who wears it but above all because the priesthood is the medium through which God's glory is made manifest in the midst of his people.

BIBLIOGRAPHY

SELECT BIBLIOGRAPHY

(An asterisk denotes works by non-Catholics)

In this series: AMIOT, François: *History of the Mass.*

ANSON, Peter F.: *Churches, Their Plan and Furnishing*, Milwaukee, Bruce, 1948.

*ATCHLEY, E. G. Cuthbert: *A History of the Use of Incense in Divine Worship* (Alcuin Club Collections), London, Mowbrays, 1909.

BISHOP, E.: *Liturgica Historica*, Oxford and New York, Oxford Univ. Press, 1918.

*COMPER, J. Ninian: *Of the Christian Altar and the Buildings which Contain It*, London, S.P.C.K., 1950.

*COX, J. C.: *English Church Fittings, Furniture and Accessories*, London, Methuen, 1934.

*DIX, Gregory: *A Detection of Aumbries*, London, Dacre Press, 1945. (See below, Van Dijk and Walker.)

GUARDINI, Romano: *Sacred Signs*, London and New York, Sheed and Ward, 1931.

JUNGMANN, Joseph Andreas, S.J.: *The Mass of the Roman Rite, its Origins and Development* (Missarum Solemnia) translated by F. A. Brunner, C.SS.R. Two volumes, New York, Benziger, 1951 and 1955; Abridged, one volume edn, revised by Charles K. Riepe, London, Burns Oates, and New York, Benziger, 1959.

KLAUSER, Theodor: *The Western Liturgy and its History*, translated by F. L. Cross, London, Mowbray, and New York, Moorhouse, 1952.

O'CONNELL, J.: *Church Building and Furnishing*, London, Burns Oates, 1955, and Notre Dame, Ind., Univ. of Notre Dame Press, 1956.

O'SHEA, William J.: *The Worship of the Church*, Westminster, Md., Newman Press, 1957.

PUNIET, Dom Pierre de: *The Roman Pontifical, A History and a Commentary*, London and New York, Longmans, 1932.

ROULIN, Dom E.: *Vestments and Vesture*, St Louis, Herder, 1931.

VAN DIJK, S. J. P., O.F.M., and WALKER, J. Hazelden: *The Myth of the Aumbry* (Notes on medieval reservation practice and eucharistic devotion with special reference to the findings of Dom Gregory Dix), London, Burns Oates, 1957.

WEBB, Geoffrey: *The Liturgical Altar*, London, Burns Oates, 1939.

The Twentieth Century Encyclopedia of Catholicism

The number of each volume indicates its place in the over-all series and not the order of publication.